LEGALLY BLIND
To The Child In The Womb

BARBARA J. GRIER

www.xulonpress.com

DEDICATION

To
The Lord Jesus Christ the author of life, and to my ancestor
whose cry for freedom ignited the fire for this book. A fire
initiated by God to now free the babe in the womb.

ENDORSEMENTS

Barbara Grier has written a powerful commentary on one of the most important issues of the day!

> Allan Parker, President, The Justice Foundation
> Lead Council for Norma McCorvey Jane Doe
> in the overturn case of Roe v. Wade
> Director Operation Outcry

Barbara has written a brilliant and powerful book supporting the sanctity of human life. She takes you into an in depth study of the ungodly reasoning of many in this world and their flimsy foundations for their support of abortion. If you're not convinced that it's both immoral and a ploy of the enemy you too may have a major paradigm shift after reading her book. Be ready to embrace life. If you weren't convinced before you will be after you read this!

> Brian & Candice Simmons
> The Passion Translation

In order to change strong opinions it takes clear and precise information that pierce through the confusion and callousness of the heart! With such an opinion deeply entrenched in the earth concerning abortion new and flesh examples and arguments must be put forth that can shine light on the subject. Barbara Grier in her new book "Legally Blind" will help people who can't see through the confusion because of media, politicians and even the silence of the church to receive their sight and common sense back in this most critical area of abortion.

Bishop Larry Jackson
Founder and Pastor of Bethel Outreach International Church in
Charlotte, NC

It's been said that abortion is the watershed issue of our generation. There is such a lack of clarity on the matter even within the church of Jesus Christ. Barbara has brought a clarity of understanding on the multiple factors connected with abortion that most only see dimly at best. Legally Blind is indeed a cure for a blindness that has affected a generation. The treatment of the subject is thorough yet the discussion of the subject is easy to comprehend and straight forward. The book brings a clear focus to a fuzzy understanding that is so common in our culture today. This is a powerful little book that contains truth that will set a generation free in knowledge of what God has to say about the subject. This is the best discussion of abortion that I have seen yet. Legally Blind is an important work and you will be awakened to the truth concerning the plague on our society that we have permitted in abortion.

Randy O'Dell, Senior Pastor, Freedom Gateway Center,
Farmington, MI

TABLE OF CONTENTS

ACKNOWLEDGEMENTS

I am very grateful for my precious friends who assisted in the mechanical completion of the manuscript: Emelina Brincat, Stella R. Calloway, Mary Patricia Nichols and my sister Elaine O. Standifer.

My dear supporters: Joyce Smith, Karin Plummer, Pam Bonk, Mary Pat Bower, my family, church and all who prayed and encouraged me to continue this assignment.

PREFACE

Written in the Declaration of Independence is this statement we have all heard "We hold these truths to be self-evident, that all men are created equal, that they are endowed by their Creator with certain unalienable Rights, that among these are Life, Liberty and the pursuit of Happiness."

Because of that statement we have understood that **life** is a guarantee for all citizens of this nation. Later the Bill of Rights guaranteed protection of those truths as basic principles of human liberty.

Yes life is a guarantee but not for the child in the womb according to Roe v. Wade the law legalizing abortion in the United States. Along with Doe v Bolton abortion is legal all nine months of pregnancy due to the health provision allowing abortion for any reason including emotional well-being.

The equal protection guaranteed for all people in the 14th amendment was denied the child in the womb. Perhaps because of the child's location, but I ask does location change the value of a human life? How can a few inches traveling down a birth canal change you into a human being?

Likewise would size, developmental level, or the fact that the child needs to depend on its parents, diminish its humanity, or its guarantee of protection under the constitution?

Now I believe in choice along with most people. We can choose our restaurants, clothes, vacations, friends, spouses and so on... However we have not been given a fundamental or natural right to choose to take another human beings life.

Regardless of the developmental elements mentioned physicians, biologists, and other scientists agree that conception marks the beginning of the life of a human being and a member of the human species.

Therefore Roe v Wade is a violation of the constitution of the United States. It has disregarded the original intent of the constitution, the founding fathers, the bill of rights, God's commandment thou shall not kill, and it has made people blind to the child in the womb.

These are the facts:
- At conception the sperm joins with the ovum and the genetic blue print of every detail of development is then present
- In 18-22 days there is a heart beat
- There are brain waves in 42 days
- In the 2nd month facial features ears, nose, lips, tongue develops
- By the 2nd month also all body systems have formed
- From now on changes are primarily in size and refinement of body parts already existing.

These are the stages of a human being, a child in the womb with a separate DNA and genetic structure.

I believe many have believed a lie like the long standing tale about ostriches burying their heads in the sand. They don't react to danger by sticking their head in the sand. Ostriches swallow sand and pebbles to help grind up food in their stomachs. This is a false myth and perhaps an example of fallacies many have believed concerning life in the womb.

I ask you to choose to read Legally Blind. I bear no personal anger or grievances only a love for life, unalienable rights ordained by God, and the original intent of the founding fathers for this land: life, liberty and the pursuit of happiness.

INTRODUCTION

E ver had an "aha" moment? Well, several years ago I experienced one that changed my perceptions about the value of life. To put it truthfully, I had a paradigm shift. One minute, I had my personal philosophies and concepts all categorized. The next minute I was shocked, then sobbing uncontrollably for the next month at the mere mention of the issue.

Yes, I had a paradigm shift and that is what this book is about. In it, I will present a different way of looking at this issue and allow you to see the world from another perspective, another mental image that will encourage you to explore your own paradigm as Albert Einstein once said we all should do.

The word *paradigm* comes from the Greek. Stephen R. Covey in *The 7 Habits of Highly Effective People* describes a paradigm like this:

> Paradigm is originally a scientific term and is more commonly used today to mean a model, theory, perception, assumption, or frame of reference. It is the way we see the world, not in terms of our visual sense

of sight, but in terms of perceiving, understanding, and interpreting." He went on to say, "a simple way to understand paradigms is to see them as maps. The map is not the territory. It is simply an explanation of certain aspects of the territory.

Each of us has many, many maps in our head that can be divided into two main categories: maps of the way things are— realities, or maps of the way things should be—values.

We interpret everything we experience through these mental maps. We seldom question their accuracy; we're usually even unaware that we have them. We simply assume that the way we see things is the way they really are or the way they should be. Our attitudes and behaviors grow out of those assumptions.

Steven Covey gives an excellent example of a paradigm shift. It occurred on a Sunday morning while on the subway in New York City. People were sitting quietly when suddenly a man and his children entered the subway car. The children were loud and rambunctious, hitting, throwing, and grabbing things.

Instantly the whole climate changed in the car. The man sat next to Steven Covey but did nothing to control his disruptive children.

Steven was so irritated at the man's insensitivity of his children running wild. Finally, he turned to the man and asked if he would please control them. The man, looking dazed, said, "Oh, you're right! I guess I should do something. We just came from the hospital and their mother just died an hour ago. I guess I don't know how to handle it either." Suddenly, Steven saw things differently. A paradigm shift!

As a result of my own "aha" moment, I've come to realize that only too often we look at things through a distorted lens that allow us to project out of our own background, experiences or lack of. We think we are seeing things the way they really are. Actually, we need a lens correction to see accurately.

I certainly did. It happened to me one day as I overheard an interview in which a young man wanted to donate money for any black woman who would abort her baby.

He explained that he had just had a baby and wanted to make sure that affirmative action policies would not eventually affect his child's future benefits.

The abortion clinic employee replied that it was her first time hearing a donation stated in that manner. She then however, giggled and said, "I understand," and accepted the donation.

Listening to the rest of the program I learned the interview was the result of an undercover operation to reveal that African Americans and other minorities were being targeted for abortions. Yes, here in America, and it was legal.

> The covert operation was repeated in seven other states and in each instance no employee declined the money. The actual recorded investigation can be heard on the Live Action website today. [1]

> As I researched I found countless verification of this abuse in our nation.

It's difficult to describe how this revelation affected me. My shock turned into rage and then mourning over the millions of babies being slaughtered in the womb. How could I have been so blind and insensitive to this act? Could our government pass a law that was actually against humanity? Are we the people so blind or maybe indifferent to the value of all life that our silent consent prevails? In addition I was struck by people's negative responses as I shared my recent revelation. Even some in my own family wondered if I had lost my mind. After all they said, abortion was legal, and some people certainty had valid reasons.

As I pursued in prayer, I realized that my revelation was no accident but a divine appointment with an assignment to be a voice for the unborn and expose the veil of blindness the law had placed over people's hearts.

It was an assignment to cause the world to look again and see their lens distortion and allow a paradigm shift to occur, to see clearly that all life is valuable from the womb to the tomb.

Thus, I now write as one who was legally blind but now I see.

Therefore, I invite you to read *Legally Blind*. Let your guard down, get a cup of coffee, and allow yourself the expansion, exploration, and shift in paradigm that perhaps awaits you. Embrace the experience! We all deserve "aha" moments.

Chapter 1

THE PIVOTAL YEAR

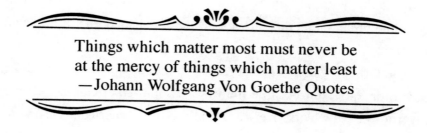

Things which matter most must never be
at the mercy of things which matter least
—Johann Wolfgang Von Goethe Quotes

The year 1973 was an interesting year. The U.S. population was 211.9 million people. A cease fire was signed ending all ground troops in Vietnam. President Nixon was investigated for the Watergate incident. Spiro Agnew resigned as vice president of the United States and pled no contest in charges to income tax evasion. Marlon Brando was named best actor for *The Godfather*. The under-employment rate was 4.9 percent, and a U.S. stamp was eight cents.

However, the most pivotal event that year and perhaps ever in this nation occurred January 23, 1973. This event allowed Americans to become legally blind to millions of babies being murdered in their mother's wombs. Yes, with the tap of the gavel seven of the nine Supreme Court justices cast a shadow over Americans by legalizing abortion in *Roe vs. Wade*. Together with the companion ruling of *Doe vs. Bolton* with health exceptions, and <u>any</u> level of distress abortions could be obtained all nine months of a pregnancy. Some call it abortion on demand.

Thus, a woman could obtain an abortion at any age (parental consent for youth under sixteen) and for any factor (physical, emotional, psychological and familial), so long as she said it was for her well-being. The well-being of the baby is not considered. Therefore, this ruling allows Americans to become legally blind to the extermination of life in the womb. It allows them to look the other way, close their eyes, and pretend that they are not aware of the shedding of innocent blood. No doubt saying it's a **law** so it's okay.

The term "legally blind" surfaced in the news in early 2008. Lt. Governor Patterson became the first African American to become governor of New York. He was legally blind. Americans rushed to their dictionaries to learn what legally blind really meant. What difficulties and handicaps were involved? Could Mr. Patterson be an effective governor for the great state of New York?

After researching his personal qualifications, we came away knowing that Governor David Patterson had soared far above his disabilities and could indeed be a great governor. However, still the concept of being legally blind is one that begs understanding for most.

The Thesaurus says it is having 20/200 vision. Your vision is 20/200 or worse in your best eye. To put it simply, a legally blind person would have to stand 20 feet from an object to see it with correct vision while a person with normal vision could stand 200 feet from the same object and experience the same acuity or keenness of vision. In Governor Patterson's case, he can only see shadows. So, he memorizes and leans heavily on his legal and professional skills.

In the case of America legalizing abortion, *Roe vs. Wade* caused the loss of acuity or keenness of sight. Like Governor Patterson whose legal blindness caused him to only see shadows, I believe a shadow was cast over the hearts of Americans, which cause us to look through a distorted lens devaluing life in the womb and becoming legally blind, blind to the fact that a person is a person no matter how small, blind to the fact that all life is valuable and precious whether it is inside or outside of the womb.

Man was created in the likeness and image of God (Genesis 1:26), and he is fearfully and wonderfully made. The prophet Jeremiah was told by God that before He formed him the womb. He knew him, approved of him, and called him to be a prophet. "Before I formed you in the womb I knew you before you were born, I set you apart" (Jeremiah 1:5).

Even science has determined that at conception a new individual comes into being, possessing a unique genetic code that determines its sex, fingerprints, hair, eye color, and facial features. [1]

At twenty-two days the baby's heart begins to beat in its own blood, and at ten weeks the baby can often be seen by ultrasound. Regardless of what you and I may look like now, we were all a one-cell organism at one time. Then we developed, as all humans do, in developmental stages. Pregnancy begins when the sperm fertilizes the female ovum (egg). A one-celled biological zygote begins, which is the first stage in human development. This zygote is biologically alive because it fulfills the four criteria needed to establish biological life: metabolism, growth, reaction to stimuli, and reproduction.

It blows my unconscionable mind to think that people say that two human begins can have sex and produce something that is not human. Some say the child is not human until he or she is out of the womb. Then what is that inhuman thing in your body? Others say it's just tissue or a blob. Again, my question is, how can two humans have a blob or tissue that is not human and all of a sudden it turns into a human in nine months? This is not a science fiction movie. Either it's human or it's not. If it is not human in the beginning, it's not going to turn into a human. Genetics doesn't work like that. A frog is a frog. A dog is a dog. A human is a human. Perhaps, if the boy or girl in the womb had fur, a tail, and a snout, its value would increase to the value of our pets. Then perhaps the babe in the womb would be priceless and very valuable.

Justice Harry Blackmun, who wrote the majority decision in *Roe vs. Wade* (1973), has argued "that the morality of abortion is completely contingent on the full humanness of the unborn." The popular arguments for abortion rights either beg the question to the full humanness of the unborn or ignore the question altogether. Both sound philosophical and scientific reasoning clearly establish the full humanness of the unborn from the moment of conception. [2]

I believe Justice Harry Blackmun is saying that there is no doubt all human life begins at conception. Yet his majority decision in *Roe vs. Wade* chooses to destroy the life of the child, establishing an unjust law, which I believe is an illegal law against nature.

I'm not encouraging anarchy or burning down abortion clinics, nor do any of my colleagues. I am saying, however, that we need to look again at the genocide this law is causing and consider the fact that it is impacting not only the United States but other nations that have followed our lead. We often send financial aid to help other nations kill their babies in the womb, and we call it humanitarian aid for women. Really, it's just extending legal blindness.

I am not a scholar of the animal kingdom, but I don't recall any animal that is known for aborting their next generation in mass. In the U.S. alone, we have aborted over fifty-six million babies since 1973, and that is only counting the ones that were reported. Many states do not report these statistics to the CDC (Center for Disease Control).

One major argument that I hear is that if we don't help women to abort their babies, they will do it anyhow and often cause great harm to themselves. We hear stories of backroom abortions and uses of coat hanger and other items used to end a pregnancy. So the alternative has been to make it legal to kill babies in the womb. This has created other harmful side effects for the woman that abortionists keep hidden. This is information women need to know before setting themselves up for unneeded wounding and pain. We will cover those unfortunate symptoms and post-abortion results in the next few chapters.

However, research has, in fact, proven that the stories of back room abortions were exaggerated and often false.

The U.S. Bureau of vital Statistics said there were only thirty-nine women who died from illegal abortions in 1972. Former medical director of Planned Parenthood, Dr. Mary Calderon, described in a 1960 , American Journal of Health article that a study in 1958 showed that 84 to 87 percent of all illegal abortions were performed by licensed physicians in good standing.

So it appears that the back alley doctors who were called "butchers" before *Roe vs. Wade* seem to automatically become legitimate doctors who now advocated for choice in 1973.

What has happened to common sense? One thing I learned as a child is that sex makes babies. My mom was old fashioned and didn't tell me much about the facts of life, only to keep my dress down, but I knew sex made babies and that made it off limits for me. (I enjoyed my life at the time and mom and dad had serious standards) If it is still true that sex makes babies, then the decision to be made is about sex; the decision is not about whether to abort. A decision to abort only comes into play after the sex act.

It is critical to understand the ramifications and possible consequences of actions and be mature enough to accept responsibilities for decisions. Abortion is not a means of birth control. Yes, sex still makes babies.

Also, so many say, "It's my body, my choice" as an excuse to abort. In reality, the baby growing in the womb is a separate human being. It is a distinct, living, and whole organism. It is not a part of a larger human being like skin cells are. Instead, it is a whole human entity capable of directing its own internal growth and development, not like somatic cells, but an embryonic human being. So the choice is focusing responsibly on sex. Or are we in America regarding sex as the new civil right? Have it any time, any way with any one and if pregnancy occurs, kill it. Is that really what we have become?

In 2004, a structured survey completed by 1,209 abortion patients at eleven large providers and in-depth interviews were conducted with thirty-eight women at four sites. Bivariate analyses examined differences in the reasons for abortion across subgroups and multivariate logistic regression models assessed associations between respondent characteristics and reported reasons.

RESULTS: The reasons most frequently cited were that having a child would interfere with a woman's education, work or ability to care for dependents (74%); that she could not afford a baby now (73%); and that she did not want to be a single mother or was having relationship problems (48%). Nearly four in ten women said they had completed their childbearing and almost one-third were not ready to have a child. Less than 1 percent said their parents' or partner's desire for them to have an abortion was the most important reason. Younger women often reported that they were unprepared for the transition to motherhood, while older women regularly cited their responsibility to dependents. [3]

Naturally we can see these are valid personal concerns impacting these women, and as a career woman myself, after looking at many of the above reasons, I would almost agree. Except, the issue is not privacy, choice, financial or economic hardship, timing, careers, family or single parenting. The issue is *what is the unborn?* Science has given clear facts that the unborn are living distinct whole human beings. Abortion thus ends the life of a human being. A living human being!

A 1981 U.S. Senate report states, Physicians, biologists, and other scientists agree that conception marks the beginning of the life of a human being—a being that is alive and is a member of the human species. There is overwhelming agreement on this point in countless medical, biological, and scientific writings. [4]

The abortion issue is not a debate between pro-choice, anti-choice, right to privacy, or trusting women. It's the answer to the question: "What is the unborn? If the unborn are not human, no justification for elective abortion is necessary. However, if the unborn are "human" no justification for elective abortion is adequate. [5]

Let's take a closer look at legal blindness.

During the early days in the U.S., it was legal to own slaves. There would be signs posted announcing slave auctions, and people would fill auction houses and bid on human beings like chattel. They would control their slaves' behavior and determine their every move. They were slaves and it was a law. They had no rights. They could be beaten, tarred and feathered, and often hung. It was a law. Yes, it was a law. But was it moral?

Would not a moral law value life? The Bible says that all men are made in the image and likeness of God. So this was a law, but was it right? Was it moral? I believe it was a law that made people legally blind to the value of human life. An inhumane act became law and people eased their conscience, looked the other way, and said, "Well, it's a law, isn't it?"

One of the major issues used to justify blacks as slaves was the issue of them being a whole person.

In 1787, the convention in Philadelphia agreed to the Three-Fifths Compromise. This became the means of determining congressional seats and tax appropriation between Northern states and Southern slave states. Each slave was counted as three fifths of a person. The law took precedence over humanity and the wicked act was justified because it became law. [6]

In the Dred Scott case of 1857, the Supreme Court declared blacks as an inferior and subordinate class. It was ruled in *Dred Scott vs. Stanford* that no one with African ancestry could claim citizenship in the United States. This case continued a precedent of injustice, prejudice, and inhumane treatment for blacks in America. [7] To solidify the subordinate class in the conscience of America, books and encyclopedias depicted slaves as half humans, having tails. This further dehumanized and enforced this unjust law. It was a massive assault on personhood that enforced people's excuse to stay legally blind.

History cannot number all of the acts of legal blindness that were forced upon the Native Americans. They were considered savages and suffered countless broken treaties. They were uprooted from their land and made to relocate on lands that could not sustain them. A tragic example of removal was the Trail of Tears.

Trail of Tears is the name given to the forced relocation and movement of Native American nations from southeastern parts of the United States following the Indian removal act of 1830. Many suffered from exposure, disease, starvation, and died on route to Oklahoma, their destination.

It was legal, but was it moral? They were dehumanized, stripped of their land and belongings. The country, being so desensitized, looked the other way because it was a law. Legal blindness!

Remember Hitler? Well, he did the same.

In 1935, the Nuremberg Law outlawed Jews from being German citizens. The next year holocausts were legalized and over four million Jews were exterminated. Cartoons routinely depicted them as pigs, dogs, rats, and other vermin. They were said to be inferior, weeds, misfits, and unequal. It was a law (and people followed it blindly), but was it moral? Had they too, become legally blind?

In the 1973 *Roe vs. Wade* case, the United States Supreme Court decided that the Right to Privacy (under the due process clause of the Fourteenth Amendment to the constitution) extends a woman the right to have an abortion. The baby boy or girl in the womb of the mother is deemed inhuman and not protected under the Fourteenth Amendment. Therefore, they could be killed. The unborn child thus has no rights.

Shockingly however, also in 1973 the Endangered Species Act was passed by congress. It legally protected hundreds of plants and animals and their young.

Perhaps you too, are not convinced that the babe in the womb is human or you may be saying it's only tissue or just another inconvenience. Perceptions often need examining. It might be time for a paradigm shift.

At one time it was thought that the earth was the center of the universe. Copernicus, however, caused a paradigm shift with his scientific revelation that the sun was the center with celestial objects revolving. Now that was an "aha" moment. Imagine the navigational nightmares that occurred at sea and the many astronomy miscalculations. However, an abortion miscalculation ends a life!

Chapter 2

RELATIVE AND NO ABSOLUTES

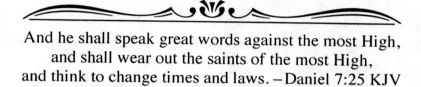

And he shall speak great words against the most High,
and shall wear out the saints of the most High,
and think to change times and laws. — Daniel 7:25 KJV

As a child I would often play various games with my friends.
When we played the game of checkers or other games, the
rules would always change. Sometimes the king could move in one
direction at their discretion but, at other times only jump back and
forth. It all depended on if they were winning or losing.

As I grew older I realized a game of checkers or any game with
them meant war. Although it was a lot of fun, I had no idea it was my
initial training in spiritual warfare, and soon, as a believer in Christ,
I was introduced to the adversary of our faith who seeks to wear out
the saints by changing times and laws.

The Book of Daniel states that Satan desires to change laws, customs, and morals so that society will align with his sinful practices
rather than releasing God's righteousness into a territory.

He is referred to as the prince of the power of the air. His purpose is to rule entire societies [John 12:31]. As a prince of this world he endeavors to hold legal right as a prince through the human sins of mankind and manipulating the structures of the world. [1]

I truly believe *Roe vs. Wade* is an example of Satan's manipulating techniques because this law has redirected attention from the life of a child in the womb to the civil rights of an adult person, which allow them the right to act as they wish regardless of the unborn child. In other words, life in the womb is relative, and its sanctity is not an absolute. So a baby in the womb is denied the absolute natural right to life if the adult has other goals.

I consider this law to be in direct opposition to the truth: truth as revealed by God before the foundation of the world, the truth that this nation has espoused for over 200 years in our courts and homes. *Roe vs. Wade* has caused people in this nation to become legally blind to the truth.

In his "Letter from a Birmingham Jail," Dr. Martin Luther King said there are two kinds of laws, just laws and unjust laws. A just law is a man-made code that squares with the moral law or the law of God. An unjust law is out of harmony with the moral law.

Any law that uplifts the human personality is just, and any law that degrades the human personality is unjust. Thus an unjust law is no law at all.

Natural law is written into the fabric of existence. That's why Thomas Jefferson said the basic principles of moral law were self-evident. In other words all men are created equal, and they are endowed by their Creator with certain unalienable rights, that among these are life, liberty and the pursuit of happiness.

Franklin D. Roosevelt said that the epidemic of world lawlessness was spreading [1882–1945]. Yes, the changing of laws and morals were evident in his day and how much more today. Lawlessness, the disregard of moral law and the expansion of unjust laws, is sweeping our nation.

We live in an era where everything is relative, and situational ethics seem to be the rule. It is a time when a person's opinion is just as good as another's and their opinions often become the rule.

In fact, moral relativism says people should do whatever they desire. There are no rights or wrongs. Everything is subjective with no absolutes.

> The problem with relativism is that if a person believes that morality is a personal definition then you surrender the possibility of making objective moral judgments about actions of others no matter how offensive they are to your sense of right or wrong. That means a relativist cannot rationally object to murder, rape, child abuse, racism, sexism or environmental destruction if those actions are consistent with the perpetrator's personal moral understanding of right or wrong. [2]

You see, we surrender the right to judge others actions, if indeed, we say right and wrong is a matter of personal choice.

If some things must be wrong and others must be right, then all things are not relative, and that concept of relativism is hypocritical and false.

Additionally, the concept of tolerance is used as a key issue in the belief of relativism. Since morals are a matter of choice, then they (according to a relativist) should be tolerated and not judged. However, if there are no rules or absolutes, how can "tolerance" now become a moral principle that, by the way, has permeated our schools, media, businesses, and nation with demands of adherence?

Stop; can you see the shift in morality? It began with a concept that your thoughts are just as good as God's or the moral code He put in the universe, which sounds like Adam and Eve all over again.

Come on—has God really said that? He really doesn't want you to know what he knows. Come on—your thoughts are just as good as His. After all aren't you gods of this earth? That sounds like the arch enemy to me. Everything is relative; there are no absolutes.

Actually, it's beyond me how the relative concept "it's my choice" has become a legitimate moral principle in our society that all must now tolerate while those who believe in morality and absolutes often are treated with disdain and not tolerated. Unfortunately, this concept has captured the minds of our nation and is inconsistent, bankrupt, and false.

Only in a world where there are absolutes can a person find true justice and peace. Otherwise, life would be meaningless and unlivable with no accountability. Adolph Hitler infiltrated Germany with beliefs like he taught in this statement: "I have freed Germany from the stupid and degrading fallacies of conscience and morality. We will train young people before whom the world will tremble." Imagine a world where that truly was the rule. The mere thought gives me the chills. I thank God for His precious guidelines for living, values within the Bible that make it clear that God does set moral laws which are the standards of right and wrong. Yes the Bible that many contest has been proven trustworthy through manuscripts, archaeological, prophetic, and statistical evidence.

Actually every good tree bears good fruit, but a bad tree bears bad fruit. Thus by their fruit you will recognize them. I believe this truth is consistent with the result of the no absolutes or moral law concept in the United States. Violent crimes have increased, birth rates of babies by unwed girls have increased, and sexually transmitted diseases have increased, while educational achievement and family stability have decreased. [Basic data from the center for disease control and department of health and human resources]

God put His moral law in sixty-six books called the Bible. It was written by forty-four authors over 1,600 years on three different continents yet with one central theme: God's love and redemption for mankind. Now, that's consistency, and that's what I need.

So what does God say in His word about unjust laws?

Well, in Isaiah 10, the Lord directed a prophecy against Judah's leaders who used their positions to unfairly enrich themselves at the people's expense. He said, "Woe to those who make unjust laws, to those who issue oppressive decrees" (Isaiah 10:1).

Again in Isaiah 45, God makes it clear that He is a God who does what is right and His word is not hidden, but true.

> I have not spoken in secret, in a dark place of the earth. I said not unto the seed of Jacob, Seek ye me in vain. I the Lord speak righteousness. I declare things that are right. (Isaiah 45:19)

Psalm 94:20–21 states, "Shall the throne of iniquity have fellowship with thee, which frames mischief by a law? They gather themselves together against the soul of the righteous and condemn the innocent blood."

The New Living Translation says it this way: "Can unjust leaders claim that God is on their side—leaders who permit injustice by their laws? They attack the righteous and condemn the innocent to death."

I believe that Psalm 94 is especially significant because it places the throne of iniquity at its focus. Now see how this unjust law connects with demonic activity to bring destruction to people in an area. This is so important to understand.

The formation of a throne of iniquity, (mentioned in Psalm 94:20–21), goes like this: first, iniquity is sin and when a certain sin like idolatry, bloodshed, immorality, and covenant breaking are committed corporately by a people in a region, gives Satan access the people and that region. He will then take advantage of that break in God's purpose, covenant, and righteous covering for that region and establishes his influence, which means injustices and crimes begin to rule the area.

Chuck Pierce continues to say in his book, *The Future War of the Church*, "From that place of influence, Satan can build a throne upon which he is seated in a territory and his dark activities among people grow and become preeminent." Revelation 2:13 states, "I know your works and you dwell where Satan's throne is."

Satan's assigned hierarchy rules from a throne built on the corporate iniquity (sin) in a region, and his throne is linked with the worship in that area. Satan knows that all men and women were created to worship and whether they realize it or not they will worship something. (Worship is serving, regarding, and esteeming another.)

The simple fact is that either they are worshipping the true and living God, or they are worshipping Satan and his demonic forces, whether overtly or through their sinful actions (whether sins of omission or commission). It is this corporate sin that builds the foundation of the throne of iniquity on which Satan is seated, and it is from that throne that the demonic forces work. [3]

In other words, demons congregate over a region and wickedly inspire people who have gained positions in society to legislate and make laws that favor Satan's agenda, like killing your unwanted baby in the womb.

Did you get that? Demons can be given power to rule through people in a region resulting from the sins of the people in that area, causing devastating human casualties.

An excellent example comes from Detroit. There was an alarming story in the Detroit news posted May 2014 that stated that around one-third of all pregnancies end in abortion. The paper reported that the city's abortion rate has been steadily climbing, hitting 31 percent in 2012. [4]

"We're seeing a picture that looks more like some third-world country than someplace in the United States," reported Susan Schooley, chairwoman of the Department of Family Medicine at a leading Detroit hospital.

Another Detroit news article by Karen Bouffar reported that women are dying from pregnancy-related causes at a rate three times greater than for the nation, resulting in a maternal death rate of 58.7per 100,000 babies—higher than Libya, Uruguay, or Vietnam.

Most recently, a June 2015 article reported that abortions in Michigan increased almost 20 percent [18.5%] from 2010 to 2015, the biggest gain of the forty-five states surveyed by The Associated Press, according to *The Detroit News*. [5]

I believe Detroit's death rate is a result of the demonic oppression influenced by the throne of iniquity (sin) in this area. When you read the news accounts of gang violence and the killing of our children in the streets, coupled with the cries of devastated families, it causes a cry within me to call on God to heal their pain and eradicate the death decree over this city.

I also believe the *Roe vs. Wade* case that promotes murdering babies in the womb, was fashioned by a throne of iniquity fueled by the shedding of innocent blood.

In other words, Satan blinded people to God's guidelines, and they chose to follow his concepts, whether overtly or subtly, whether for convenience, popularity, sensuality, or greed. They adopted his mindset and legislated the law that opposed God and His law and chose to murder innocent life in the womb. Satan changes laws just as Daniel 7 states causing legal blindness in people to the sanctity and beauty of every human being regardless of their location or status.

Legal blindness is also consistent with what occurred with the Native Americans, slavery, the Jewish Holocaust, and now, the slaughter of the unborn. It is an immoral, unjust, unrighteous act depriving precious people of their life, liberty, and pursuit of happiness. It's not relative, it's not tolerance; it is murder, and I believe it's just wrong.

Is there a comparison?

When we compare the law of God to *Roe vs. Wade*, there is really no comparison.

God's law is pure, consistent, without partiality, enduring, unchangeable, righteous, and just. God's law is based on love for every human being. Psalm 19:7 says, "the law of the Lord is perfect." and Romans 7:12 says, "the law (God's law) is holy, just, and good." It is inherent in creation and obedience brings success.

Conversely, the best way to compare the abortion law with God's law and its formation process is to share a portion of a speech made by Supreme Court Justice Scalia in 2005.

"We are in the era of the evolving Constitution," expressed Justice Antonin Scalia.

First, an evolving constitution is reinterpreting old laws to mean new things. For instance, there is no text in the constitution that you could reinterpret a right to abortion. So you need something else. The something else is called the doctrine of Substantive Due Process, which guarantees no one can be deprived of life, liberty, or property without "due process of law."

The Court says there are some liberties that are so important that no process will suffice to take them away. So when the doctrine of substantive due process was initially announced, it was limited in this way. The Court said it embraces only those liberties that are fundamental to a democratic society and rooted in the traditions of the American people.

Then, however, that limitation was eliminated. Within the last twenty years, we now have found to be covered by due process, the right to abortion, which was so little rooted in the traditions of the American people that it was criminal for 200 years. Also, the right to homosexual sodomy, which was so little rooted in the traditions of the American people, that is was criminal for 200 years," said Justice Scalia.

Okay, if you're following me, it's easy to see where the Court jumped the track. The Court has essentially liberated itself from the text of the Constitution and even from the traditions of the American people. It is now up to the Court to say what is covered by substantive due process. Thus, the nine judges on the court can cause the

Constitution to mean whatever they say. It is now flexible. Let's go further in the speech by Judge Scalia.

> "My Constitution is a very flexible Constitution," said Judge Scalia. "You think the death penalty is a good idea—persuade your fellow citizens and adopt it. You think it's a bad idea—persuade them the other way and eliminate it. You want a right to abortion—create it the way most rights are created in a democratic society, persuade your fellow citizens it's a good idea and enact it. You want the opposite—persuade them the other way. That's flexibility."

In Judge Scalia's final comments he said,

> "And finally, this is what I will conclude with, although it is not on a happy note. The worst thing about the Living Constitution is that it will destroy the constitution... this is new—50 years old or so—the Living constitution stuff. We have not yet seen what the end of the road is. I think we are beginning to see. And what it is should really be troublesome to Americans who care about a Constitution that can provide protections against majoritarian rule." [6]

In my opinion, that's a paradigm shift in the wrong direction. Look at what has happened; originally interpreting the Constitution was to begin with the text and to give the text the meaning that it bore when it was adopted by the people. It was not flexible or living, but a legal document and like all legal documents it said what it said and no more or no less. I agree with Justice Scalia. This living constitution is destroying the Constitution that we know and love.

Allan Parker of the Justice Foundation stated that 'Justice Antonin Scalia was a champion of the original text of the United States Constitution. He was also a champion for the principle that *Roe v. Wade* was wrongly decided and should be overturned. [7]

That is why *Roe vs. Wade* is an immoral, unjust law that does not consider and is actually blind to the sanctity of life. It is a law based on the opinions of man. Man is subject to changes of opinion just like the stock market fluctuates. Roe is an excellent example of relativism, morality based on the cultural trend of the day with selective rights and wrongs, no absolutes, unless of course, a negative incident affects them. Then they cry foul.

God's law does not evolve nor is it based on the fleeting opinions of man. It is unchangeable. Like God, it is the same yesterday, today, and forever.

Psalm 119:116 says, "The entirety of your word is truth and every one of your righteous judgments endures forever. Psalm 97:26 says, "Righteousness and judgment are the habitation of His throne."

Although man believes his beliefs and opinions are relative, God does not, and there are consequences when God's laws are violated, including natural and spiritual consequences that we will address.

Chapter 3

HUMAN BUT NOT A PERSON, HMM!

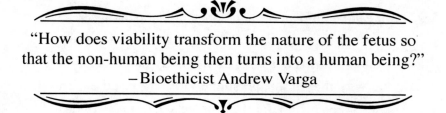

"How does viability transform the nature of the fetus so
that the non-human being then turns into a human being?"
– Bioethicist Andrew Varga

In the case of *Roe vs. Wade*, the Supreme Court basically said we know when life begins, but we must decide at what point in the development of that life, we, as a society, will confer rights of personhood, the most fundamental of which is the right to not be slaughtered. In other words, whether a human being is classified as a person depends upon how we see or value them or determine viability." [1]

In its 1859 report on criminal abortion, the American Medical Association (AMA) understood that the independent and actual existence of the child, before birth, as a living being was a scientific truth. Nothing has changed that truth for 150 years.

Even bioethicist Andrew Varga pointed out problems with the viability criterion. He asked, "How does viability transform *the nature* of the fetus so that the non-human being then turns into a human being?" He continued to say, viability is a measure of the sophistication of our neonatal life-support systems. Humanity remains the same, but viability changes. Viability measures medical technology, not one's humanity. [2]

However, it appears that in today's society, humanity is looked upon differently than personhood. The humanity of the unborn child is a matter of objective science, but personhood is a legal status society can confer upon or withhold from a class of human beings as a function of their subjective values that ultimately forms our "politics." You can be human, but not considered a person.

> Dominant societies have traditionally been selfish in the way they grant personhood. Ours is no exception. When a vulnerable group gets in our way or has something we want, we tend to define personhood in terms which exclude them. Native Americans got in the way of Westward settlement so we said they were subhuman to justify taking their land. We wanted the uncompensated work product of Blacks so we said they were subhuman to justify taking their freedom. Unborn children have gotten in the way of our 'liberation' so we say they are subhuman to justify taking their lives. [3]

Do we now have a morality based on convenience in America? Will we call an act a positive good so long as it is comfortable, brings merit, or provides financial profit? Will that action then become a law and the new moral code? As we ponder this scenario, wouldn't it open doors to lying, stealing, cheating, breaking vows, and even murder? Would following the carnal appetite of convenience (if it feels good, do it) lead us all down the road of moral collapse? Are we becoming the modern day Sodom and Gomorrah?

I believe a new moral code is emerging in our nation. Those 18-24 called Mosaics and my age group Baby Boomers when put side by side statistics soar. Mosaics are more likely to have sex outside of marriage, get drunk, lie and use porn. Often this evolution we are experiencing is viewed regularly in our culture.

Walter B. Hoye II states, "We no longer have to wonder whether morality based on convenience is a positive good or positive evil, whether or not it frees us or enslaves us, whether or not it brings us life or death. Morality based on convenience clearly speaks for itself."[4]

According to Webster's dictionary the word *morals* means having the principle of right or wrong behavior. Unlike animals, which don't have a moral code of conduct and are not responsible for their behaviors, human beings were created as moral creatures.

God handed down moral guidelines to Moses in the book of Exodus (Exodus 20). Although the Supreme Court outlawed their usage in the public schools in the mid-1960s, they were meant to be a blessing and a moral guideline to show us how to live. Just think of everyone obeying the sixth commandment that you shall not murder and the eighth commandment that you shall not steal. Our world would nearly be free of crime—no need for any jails! Furthermore, over 56 million aborted babies in the U.S. would be here to pay taxes and aid the economy. How many potential doctors, lawyers, teachers, and presidents have been slaughtered at the altar of convenience? How can we judge from conception what value was purposed for that life on the earth?

For instance, let's consider this situation: There is a preacher and his wife who are very poor. They already have fourteen children and now she finds out she's pregnant with the fifteenth child. They are living in poverty. Considering their poverty and the world population, should they abort?

What about this situation? The father is sick with a bad cold and the mother has tuberculosis. They have had four children already. The first is blind, the second died, the third is deaf, and the fourth has tuberculosis. She is pregnant again. Would you recommend abortion?

What about this situation? A white man has raped a thirteen year old black girl and she is pregnant. If you were her parents, would you consider recommending abortion?

Had you chosen abortion in the first case you would have killed John Wesley, founder of the Methodist church. If you would have chosen abortion in the second situation, you would have aborted Ludwig Von Beethoven. If you would have aborted in the third, you would have aborted gospel singer Ethel Waters who wrote "His Eye is on the Sparrow."

Dear one, the right of life and death should remain in the hands of Almighty God. These are just a sample of those destined to impact and change our world. Look at what the world would have been denied had these lives been silenced because of legal blindness.

Thomas Kuhn, an American physicist and philosopher of science said, "All significant breakthroughs were a break with old ways of thinking. America, let's think again!

According to scripture every person existed in the spirit realm before their entrance to earth. In Jeremiah 1:5, the Lord told Jeremiah that before He formed him in the womb, He knew him. That word *knew* meant a personal awareness and relationship. The Message

Bible puts it like this: "Before I shaped you in the womb, I knew all about you, before you saw the light of day, I had holy plans for you. A prophet to the nations. That's what I had in mind for you."

Also, Ephesians 1:4 states, "According as he hath chosen us in Him before the foundation of the world" and verse 5 says, "having predestinated us unto the adoption of children."

To put it simply, God knew and had a prior relationship in the spirit realm with every human being. His love created them and ordained them for a time and purpose. Thus there are no throw-away babies and no one is an accident. They are all sacred and precious in God's sight.

Psalm 139:13 says, "For you have created my inmost being, you knit me together in my mother's womb. I am fearfully and wonderfully made."

Imagine the joy Elizabeth experienced when the babe leaped in her womb at the acknowledgment of Jesus snuggled in the womb of His mother Mary (Luke 1:44). My, what a moment that was!

Unfortunately there is an enemy that would kill destroy or abort all of our lives if he had a chance. Thankfully there was a divine protective Hand over our lives or I would not be writing today and you would not be reading. Selah! (Pause and reflect)

Chapter 4

THE BLOOD HAS A VOICE

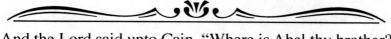

And the Lord said unto Cain, "Where is Abel thy brother?
And he said, "I know not, am I my brother's keeper? And
God said, "What hast thou done? The voice of thy brother's
blood cries unto me from the ground." –Gen. 4:9-10 KJV

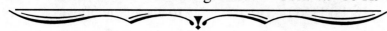

I thank God for the sacrifice of His Son's blood that redeems mankind. Satan, who is a counterfeiter, however, uses the murder of innocent lives as a blood sacrifice that fuels his immoral and evil work in the earth. In Genesis 4, God told Cain the voice of the blood of his brother Abel, (whom he murdered) cried out from the grave. God is not referring to the audible sound of Abel's voice but the sound that resonated from his blood. That sound is life: Leviticus 17:11 says, "For the life of the flesh is in the blood."

Yes, life is in the blood and it has a sound. Everything has sound. According to the American Heritage Dictionary, "**Sound** is a **mechanical wave** that is an **oscillation** of **pressure** transmitted through a **solid liquid** or **gas**, composed of **frequencies** within the range of hearing."[1] That simply means that blood also has a sound and God could hear the sound of slain Abel's voice of life crying out from the earth, life that sprang forth from the blood.

Later the Lord told Noah in Genesis 9:4, after the flood, to be fruitful and multiply. They could eat every moving thing on earth for meat, but could not eat blood, for the life of that animal was in the blood.

We all know when the blood of a person or animal is withdrawn, the person dies. Why? The source of its life flows through the blood. We've heard convicted murderers in movies say; "I have blood on my hands." What they are really saying is, "I took a person's life!"

So, when God said that Abel's blood cried out from the ground, it was the very life in his blood that was crying out. The spirit of his life within his blood was responding to his murder. It was that cry of anguish and loss that touched the heart of God. God had been robbed, robbed of His expression on earth through Abel.

Noah was further warned by God that whosoever shed man's blood, by man shall his blood be shed, for in the image of God made He man (Genesis 9:6).

No doubt you see the chain of events that would occur as a result of the shedding of innocent blood. The murder of the innocent would cause repetitive murders in the earth of millions, even billions, crying out from the ground. Innocent blood in the image of God is crying out for *vengeance*, vengeance for a life stolen!

Certainly our nation can bear witness to the escalating murders occurring in our land. More than fifty six million aborted babies' voices are crying out from the ground in America. Can you hear the life within their blood crying their lost destinies? Listen, can you identify the doctors, nurses, attorneys, police officers, and many more precious ones lost forever, lost because of the choice of legal blindness?

Praise God, however, when Jesus died on Calvary, He bore and paid for the sins of mankind, and His blood cries out louder for FORGIVENESS AND PARDON. Yes, the blood still speaks. Hebrews 12:24 states, "Jesus the mediator of the new covenant and to the blood of sprinkling that speaketh better things than the blood of Abel." The God mandate was not to kill innocent life.

However, the children of Israel were slow learners because this law was breached often, but not without consequences.

In the book of Leviticus 20, the Lord said to Moses concerning the Israelites,

> "Moreover, you shall say to Israelites, any one of the Israelites or the strangers that sojourn in Israel who gives any of his children to Moloch (the fire god worshipped with human sacrifices) shall surely be put to death, the people of the land shall stone him with stones.
>
> I will also set My face against that man (opposing him, withdrawing My protection from him and excluding him from my covenant) and will cut him off from among his people because he has given his children to Moloch, defiling My sanctuary and profaning My holy name."

As you can see, the law was written with the punishment attached. Israel had been seduced into following the practice of child sacrifice.

They would take their infant child and place it in the arms of a burning idol and sacrifice it to the demonic god, Moloch. Their consequence was as the Lord had told Noah in Genesis 9:6, "whosoever sheds the blood of man by man shall his blood be shed, for in the image of God was man made." They were to be stoned, but if the people refused to stone them and just winked or ignored them, God then would turn His face against them and cut them off from Him and His people. The consequence here was death if they murdered their innocent child. Legal blindness was not an option!

The Lord is very adamant about shedding the blood of innocent life. Why? Because doing this defiles and pollutes the land. Numbers 35:33 says, "Do not pollute the land where you are." Bloodshed pollutes the land and atonement cannot be made for the land on which blood was shed except by the one who shed it (NIV).

In other words the land remains unclean until the blood of the murderer is shed. You see the crime is not only an offense against the sanctity of life, but it also pollutes the land.

In the case of *Roe vs. Wade* and the corporate sin of America aborting over fifty-five million babies, that same number of fifty-six million lives would be required in payment for those murdered in the womb, if, of course, the math is taken literally. God is a loving God. Thankfully, He sent Jesus to make atonement for sin. If man would turn and repent today, God would forgive and heal the land.

Looking back to Leviticus 20, the Lord withdrew His hand of *protection from those who sacrificed their children to Moloch. Could this be the reason why America is facing so many calamities before and since 9/11?*

Has God just stepped back, His protective covering gone? Is He delaying major judgment in mercy waiting for us to repent and turn back to Him? After all, many American's believed our foundation was, *"in God we trust." I always did!*

Do we reverently fear God and His word? Do we love what He loves and hate what He hates? Or have we equated His desire and Word to the opinions of corruptible man?

If that is a different perspective for you, please consider it deeply. Reverence for who God is and His Word will open up treasures of wisdom and knowledge beyond your expectations.

In the book, *The Harbinger*, Jonathan Cahn shares a series of nine signs that appeared in ancient Israel warning of destruction that are now appearing in America. The book compellingly implores America to return to God before its future is devastatingly altered.

The book of Jeremiah has many instances in which the prophet, weeping, begged Israel to repent of its wicked ways and return to God. Their hearts, being captivated with evil, would not permit them to turn. Jeremiah 17:10 says, "I the Lord search the heart; I try the reins, even to give every man according to his ways and according to the fruit of his doings."

Friend, *Roe vs. Wade* is an assault on the life of every child, and their spilled blood defiles the land, as well as causes America to be aligned for judgment from a Holy God. A vessel ordained for Him to occupy now silenced forever. Legal blindness has severe consequences—lives now silenced forever.

Our human body is God's home.

"A body has thou prepared for me," are the words Jesus spoke to His Father, (Hebrews 10:5). Yes, a body overshadowed by the Holy Spirit was placed in the womb of a chosen virgin.

A human body was destined to be the dwelling place of Jesus, who would ultimately sacrifice and offer His life for the salvation of the world.

God has always desired a dwelling place with man. Man was created in His image and likeness and dwelled with the Almighty before the foundation of the world. Jeremiah was told, "I knew you before I formed you in the womb and before you came forth I sanctified you and ordained you a prophet to the nations."

Prophetically, 1,500 years before the body of Jesus was formed in the Virgin Mary, the Lord told Moses to build Him a sanctuary, a dwelling place so he could dwell with His people. That sanctuary was the tabernacle of Moses, and it also took nine months to erect. Yes nine months! Kevin Conner says in his book, *The Tabernacle of Moses*, "when we compare — Exodus 19:1 and Numbers 9:1 with the tradition in Jewish history, we find that the tabernacle took approximately nine months to complete. After nine months it became the habitation of God."[2]

Interestingly, everything has design and purpose in God's economy. The natural things often point to the spiritual. The body of Jesus took nine months to miraculously form in Mary's womb. God purposed also that every child conceived in the womb would become a promise dwelling place for Him. Our body would be His dwelling place, He would occupy and minster to the world through. This theme goes from Genesis to Revelations. Colossians 1:16 states that everything was made by God and for God and by Him does everything consist (my paraphrasing).

The Lord also placed His sign on the inside of every human body called laminin. Laminin is the cell adhesion molecule that holds the human body together. It's a chain of molecules that is shaped like the cross! Did you get that? The sign of the cross has been formed inside your human body through a chain of molecules! It's the glue of the human body. It holds your skin, bones, organs and every part of your body together so you won't fall apart. That is awesome!

Everyone born is fearfully and wonderfully made by and for our God. God said He would never leave us or forsake us! He would hold us in the palms of His hand and our walls would be forever before Him. Yes, He, God would hold us together. That's awesome!

Every human body prepared in the womb of a woman has a purpose and destiny regardless of the circumstances surrounding the conception. If life was the result of the sexual encounter, then that life had been predetermined by God before the foundation of time.

Let us pray:

Lord God, please forgive us for shedding the innocent blood of millions of babies in the womb. They are crying out their purposes from the ground. The life within the blood SPEAKS!

You are a God who makes and keeps covenant. The blood covenant you made with each child in the womb has a voice that cries and awaits restitution. Clean our lens and cause keenness of vision to recognize and value life in the womb as you do. Lord, please forgive us if through our ignorance and disobedience of your laws we opened the door for Satan's evil work to advance in our land. Break every chain and wrong mindset that opposes your Word and set us free. Again forgive and cleanse us through the Blood of Your Son Jesus Christ, His blood that speaks FORGIVINESS! Amen!

Chapter 5

BATTLE FOR THE SEED

How art thou fallen from heaven,
O Lucifer, son of the morning!
How art thou cut down to the ground,
Which did weaken the nations!
Isaiah 14:12 KJV

We begin this chapter with the fall from heaven that changed history, the fall of Lucifer from his illustrious position as son of the morning. He was not content to be the anointed cherub that covered God's holy mountain. His pride and ambition caused him to want more. He wanted to be God and his words reveal the condition of his heart. Isaiah 14:12–14 says:

For thou hast said in thine heart,

I will ascend into heaven,

I will exalt my throne above the stars of God;

I will sit also upon the mount of the congregation,

In the sides of the north; I will ascend above the heights of the clouds;

I will be like the most High. Yet thou shalt be brought down to hell,

To the sides of the pit. (Isaiah 14: 12–15)

Even after being tossed out of heaven, Lucifer, now Satan, continued his plan of exaltation to be like God. His strategy is to battle for the seed of mankind. He is determined to sabotage, compel, or capture the seed of man to establish his evil kingdom on earth.

Referred to as the prince of the power of the air (Ephesians 2: 1–2) he commands the evil forces of darkness and wickedness in the heavens. He and his evil forces tempt and convince man to commit sin to empower his evil reign.

We thank God that Satan was dealt a blow at the cross by Jesus' victory. We know through the Word of God that the Lord will eradicate Satan completely and usher in a new heaven and earth where righteousness will reign supreme forever (Revelation 20: 10, 21:11).

However, until then the battle for the seed of mankind continues. Let's look at several accounts of the enemy's pursuit, strategy and then fall in this battle.

There was a woman named Jochebed. The name means "Yahweh's glory." Names have such significance. Many names I hear today cause me to wonder what the person's future will be. For instance, think of calling your child Ichabod, "the glory has departed" or Lo-Ammi "Not my people." Wow! Names can show relationship, point to destiny, speak of one's character, title, position, or distinction. Names are so very important, like Benjamin, "son of my right hand." Jochebed's name, "Yahweh's glory," suggested to me that the bearer of this name had a special relationship with Yahweh God. Her presence, no doubt, was poignant with the essence of God. She had a sweet disposition and the aroma of incense followed her. You would be attracted to her and welcome her presence because God's love flowed from her. No wonder God chose her to be the mother of the deliverer (Moses) He was sending to set His people free from Egyptian bondage.

She lived, however, in dangerous times. The enemy wanted to destroy the seed of the next generation, and he was going to use the King of Egypt.

In time the Israelites had grown and experienced much prosperity, but a new pharaoh who became fearful of the Israelites' numbers began to oppress them with hard labor. The oppression caused the Israelites to cry out to God.

God knows how to get our attention, doesn't He? What was God up to? Maybe they had become too satisfied with the leeks and garlic and their good life or maybe they had become complacent or perhaps it was just time for them to leave Egypt. After all, it was Canaan that had been promised to them, not Egypt. The season had changed. It was time for a shift. Now often times during a shift, something is being divinely birthed.

God is bringing about a new order, a new priesthood, and a new direction. In this case, it was someone being birthed. It was a child who would lead God's people into their next level of covenant faith and preserve the generational seed.

Make no mistake: the devil has always wanted to destroy the seed. It started in the garden with Eve (Genesis 3:15). The enemy's plots and strategies will continue until Jesus returns. We must wake up to his plan.

So they cried out to God, "Help us, don't you see what pharaoh is doing to us?" Of course, God saw it! How many times have you and I experienced oppression and cried out to God only to find out that He had another plan? It was transition time. He was initiating a shift. It was time to move. Although we may not yet see it, in due time, it would manifest. God's ways are perfect.

So the Israelites found themselves in a perfect storm. Jochebed was a key component because she had to have the ear to hear from God and navigate around the enemy's strategy to destroy her seed, Israel's inheritance. In an attempt to eradicate the Hebrew people, pharaoh ordered the Hebrew midwives to throw all male babies into the Nile River, an unjust law! However, the midwives feared God and did not comply. Just think of it. They were ordered to kill the seed of their next generation. It's like the Irish would kill the seed of Irishmen or Latinos would kill the seed of Latinos or African Americans would kill the seed of African Americans. Thus destroy their legacy.

Thank goodness the midwives feared God and told pharaoh that the Hebrew women were not like others. They gave birth before the midwives arrived.

God rewarded the midwives for honoring Him. Acts 45:29 says, "It's better to obey God than man." as Apostle Peter expounded when facing the Sanhedrin for using the name of Jesus when they were in the synagogue. So Jochebed had her child, and he was a goodly child, the scripture states. Since his life was in danger, she decided to hide him for three months, muzzling his cries at night with her lullabies and during the day allowing his older siblings extra loud play times.

In Psalm 27:5 David says in the day of trouble God will hide him in his shelter. In the secret place of his tent will he hide me? He will set him high on a rock, (Amplified Bible version). God is our hiding place and protection from the enemy. He will cover the enemy's eyes until he is ready for your unveiling.

Soon it was obvious that Jochebed could no longer hide her baby. What would she do now? Legal blindness was never a thought.

I believe it was God who inspired her to take the next daring step. She would prepare a basket and apply tar and pitch to waterproof it. Then she would place the child in it and set it among the reeds on the bank of the Nile River. Then his sister would watch to see what would happen to him.

Imagine the beating of her heart, the perspiration on her brow, as she awaited the report from her daughter. What would become of her son? Her husband was waiting prayerfully by her side. Suddenly, the tent door swung open and in ran Marian, her daughter. She learned that pharaoh's daughter had come to the river to bathe. When she saw the basket, she ordered her slave girl to bring it to her. When she opened the basket, the babe cried, igniting her compassion for him. Marian emerged and asked if she would like to have a nurse, and she agreed.

Jochebed answered the call and received wages to nurse her own child. In contrast, I wonder how many midwives or women would have done what the king demanded? How precious were their children to them? Because of Jochebed's obedience, a nation was delivered through the birth of a child.

Each human is fearfully and wonderfully made, as David indicated in Psalm 139: 13–15: "My substance was not hid from thee, when I was made in secret when you knit me together in my mother's womb." David praised God for the awesome wonder of his birth. To know that before we were formed, God knew us in the spirit, way before our dad had a twinkle in his eye toward our mother. In other words, before our conception, we were known by Almighty God. Again, we are no accident!

Thus, Moses was sent as a seed to the earth to deliver the children of Israel from Egyptian bondage. Like Moses we were also known by God before we were born, given an assignment and purpose. That certainly confirms the sanctity of every life. Every child is a human being born in the image and likeness of God, who God Himself has chosen, separated, and appointed a purpose in the earth. That speaks of great value. We are chosen and accepted in the beloved.

When I think of value, acceptance, and being chosen, I cannot help but think of Queen Esther. She and her kinsmen were taken into exile from her home in Jerusalem to Persia. When her parents died, her cousin Mordecai adopted her, and she became his daughter. While living in Shushan, King Ahasuerus banished his queen for disobeying him. So he commanded that young maidens be brought to his palace to look for a new queen. Esther was one of them. She was beautiful, charming, and lovely to look at; no wonder she gained the favor of the head eunuch immediately.

Each maiden received beauty treatments. For twelve months the maidens were treated with sweet spices, perfumes, and other items of beautification. Then the maidens were taken to the king at night and would return the next morning. Then whoever he called for again would become queen. Esther received grace and favor in the king's sight and she became his bride, Queen of Shushan, the royal city of Persia. What a privilege for a little Jewish orphan girl.

Meanwhile, her cousin Mordecai was serving at the palace as a guard. He had instructed Esther not to reveal her nationality. She had kept his word as she did growing up. This was excellent advice because around that time the king promoted Haman, the Agagite, to be Prime Minister, and everyone was to bow in reverence as he passed by. No kidding! Bow and he wasn't even the king. Well, no doubt this went to his head, because when he learned that Mordecai did not bow, he was furious. He devised a plan to get rid of Mordecai and all of the Jews. Now I wonder why he wanted to get rid of all the Jews. Could it be that there was a generational hatred between the Agagites and the Jews? Yes, there could be. Holman's Bible Dictionary says that Agagite is probably a synonym for Amalekite people.

Amalekites were the first to attack Israel after the Exodus at Rephidim (Numbers 34:29), and God eventually commanded their extermination. So, it is no wonder when he heard that Mordecai was a Jew, he plotted his demise along with his people. What was his plan? I love detective stories that you have to figure out why the act was committed, or better yet, who did it.

Well, we have the motive, and we know that Haman is going to commit a heinous deed. What was his scheme? Well, Haman simply went to the king and lied. He said there were people living in Shushan who did not regard the king or his laws and they should be destroyed. He advised the king that on a certain day, one year hence, every man, woman and Jewish child should be killed and those who executed the killing could take their property. He even told the king that he would donate 10,000 talents of silver to the treasury.

It was a law, written and signed by the king and delivered by his messengers. It was a law, and any non-Jew could now commit murder and take possession of their victim's property. After all, laws are to be obeyed. It was legal.

Think for a moment of the people who would begin sizing up their Jewish neighbors to see who they could gain the most from after their murder. Will it be the neighbor on the right or the neighbor on the left?

However, let's ponder this a little further. Can a piece of paper signed and sealed by the king as law cause people to ignore the morality of that law? Yes, it's a law, but is it moral? Has this law made them legally blind to the morality of the issue? Does being a government law make it right? Could they violate their conscience by fulfilling a law because it is government sanctioned? Think about it. If so, have they become legally blind? Has the law given them an excuse to commit a deed or sanction a deed that they know is immoral? But it's legal, so can they just look the other way, ignore morality, and do the deed? Is there a higher law? A moral law? Is it possible to become legally blind and not realize it or not admit it?

Needless to say, Mordecai and the Jews in Shushan put on sackcloth and ashes and began to mourn their plight.

Word came to Esther that her uncle was at the palace gate in sackcloth and ashes. She probably thought first, "Has he lost his mind? I'm the queen. Why would he come to the palace looking like that?" So she sent a change of clothes to him to change into. But Mordecai refused and sent word of Haman's plot to kill the Jews and asked her to go to the king.

Esther responded that she had not been summoned in thirty days, so she would risk death by going. Mordecai responded that perhaps this was why she had become queen.

Challenged, Esther complied, ordered a fast and went before the king. He granted her request. Haman was hanged on the very gallows he prepared for Mordecai. A decree was sent to reverse the law that ordered the Jews murdered.

I admire both Mordecai and Esther for allowing God to position them strategically for His use. Regardless of the circumstances, they stood. Mordecai exemplified such wisdom and insight. He was a dedicated man of God and a precious father to Esther, one who stood in the gap and gave guidance in the midst of adversity.

Esther, indeed, had come to the kingdom for just such a time. Others had returned to Jerusalem after the exile, but her family had remained in Persia, no doubt divinely led to avert the plan of Haman.

There is a call in the Spirit for the Mordecais and Esthers of today to arise and come forth. We need fathers like Mordecai who will, if necessary, adopt, cover, protect, inspire, and guide the Esther's of today; those who God is calling forth to deliver His people from oppression, who will become Christ's bride walking in intimacy and sanctification before him, who will arise and shout to the enemy "NOT ON MY WATCH!" No, you're not going to take my family, my church or my nation and you're going to stop stealing our babies before they are born. Your time is up! "We take authority over your works in the name of Jesus Christ of Nazareth!"

Arise Esther's, it's your time. It's time to walk in dominion. Taking back everything the enemy has stolen, possessing the promises of God and refusing to be legally blind.

Both the story of Jochebed and Esther indicate what God will do to preserve innocent life. After all, His aim is to preserve His seed, hidden in each body, ordained to display His image in the earth.

Chapter 6

THE KEY THAT UNLOCKS

We do not want word to go out that we want to exterminate the Negro population and the minister is the man who can straighten out that idea if it ever occurs to any of their more rebellious members.
— Margaret Sanger's Letter to C. J. Gamble

*W*hat is the key that unlocks the mystery to the high rate of abortions in the black community? There is truly a strategy destroying the seed of black America. However, let's first review those abortion statistics.

Since 1973 abortion killed more Black Americans than all the other leading causes of death combined; more than cancer, crime, accidents, heart attacks, and Aids. The abortion rate for black women is almost 4 times that of white women, in the United States. [1] On average 870 black babies are aborted every day in the United States. This has greatly impacted the population levels of African Americans in the United States. [2] Since 1973 nearly 30% of the black population was erased through abortion. (Bound 4 Life)

More than 16 million black babies have been aborted since the 1973 Roe v Wade Supreme court decision. Black women make up only about 14 percent of the female population, but abort 36.2 percent of all abortions in the United States. For every 1,000 live births, non-Hispanic black women had 459 abortions, while non-Hispanic white women had 132 abortions per 1,000 live births. [3]

In Michigan where I reside, Black women had 13,065 (49.6 %) of the 26,321 abortions performed on Michigan residents in 2014. Of the total 27,629 reported abortions in Michigan in 2014, 1,308 were performed on non-residents and 26,321 were performed on residents.

Black women make up only 14 percent of Michigan female population, yet they had 49.6 percent of all abortions recorded in the state in 2014. [4] African Americans are no longer the nation's largest minority group. Hispanics have outpaced blacks in population growth.

What is the root of these high numbers? I was perplexed until one day, while typing with the television on in the background; I heard an interviewer talk about the abortion issues and how African Americans were targeted by the strategic placing of the majority of clinics in minority neighborhoods.

I heard that Margaret Sanger and her Birth Control League, now known as Planned Parenthood, encouraged extermination of those she deemed unfit in society. She instituted the Negro Project in 1926, which enlisted black ministers and leaders to encourage black women to abort their babies, supposedly to make their lives easier. Not only were there abortions, but also sterilizations as a means to limit the black population in the nation.

This so sparked my interest that I investigated further and found the following.

In a letter to a supporter, Margaret Sanger said,

> "To avoid the appearance of extermination, let's have
> their black leaders convince them that because they
> are poor this is the best thing for them." Margaret
> Sanger was a Eugenicist! In her book, Pivot of
> Civilization, she said, "Blacks are weeds, reckless
> breeders who should never have been born and are
> unfit to have children."

The eugenicist plan was to identify so-called defective family trees and subject them to lifelong segregation and sterilization programs to kill their bloodlines. They were going to wipe away their reproductive capability because they deemed them weak, inferior, and unfit. Interestingly, *the eugenics theory was created in 1863 by Sir Francis Galton, a cousin of Charles Darwin.*

Even the United States Supreme Court endorsed aspects of eugenics. In a 1927 court decision, Supreme Court Justice Oliver Wendell Holmes wrote,

> It is better for the entire world, if instead of waiting
> to execute degenerate offspring for crime or to let
> them starve for their imbecility, society can prevent
> those who are manifestly unfit from continuing their
> kinds... three generations of imbeciles are enough.

This decision opened the floodgates for thousands to be coercively sterilized or otherwise persecuted as subhuman. Years later, the Nazis, at the Nuremberg trials, quoted Justice Holmes' words in their own defense. [5]

Can you imagine how that information made my blood curl? Where had I been?

Why was I so oblivious to this plot against black people? So I eagerly delved into researching this issue more. I learned that after the emancipation of slavery, the question arose in the nation of what to do with three million black people.

That question was soon answered by the Supreme Court with the *Dred Scott* case in 1857 and *Plessey vs. Ferguson* case in 1896. They declared black people an inferior and subordinate people who could not become citizens. That decree was not changed or disputed and neither was the practice of prejudice and discrimination challenged toward blacks.

One hundred years later, with the Civil Rights Bill of 1964, discrimination and segregation laws were addressed, but the inferiority decree that released a curse upon black identity for generations remained.

In 2009 149 years after Lincoln signed the Emancipation Proclamation the U.S. Senate in unanimous voice vote apologized to African Americans for slavery and the racial discrimination during the Jim Crow era. The House of Representatives apologized the prior year. The event was not widely published, and a disclaimer regarding reparations was included.

This disheartens me when I recall the reparations the government awarded Native Americans, Japanese Americans, and other ethnic people for injustices they sustained. This inferior and subordinate decree of identity has still stereotyped black people in America and fueled and supported institutional racism for generations.

Institutional racism is a system of procedures and patterns in all walks of life, such as education, media, government, religion, employment, sports, housing, and so on that entertained discrimination policies toward one group of people while another group maintained the power, influence, respect, and well-being in society over the other.

It is more subtle than individual racism but very destructive to humanity. Because power is a necessary precondition, it depends on the ability to give or withhold social benefits, facilities, services, and opportunities from someone who should be entitled to them and are denied on the basis of race, color, or national origin. [6]

This policy also supported the indoctrination system that Willie Lynch, who was a slave owner, said in 1712, which would last and be self-refueling for three hundred or more years. The slave owners were to break black people as you would a horse and instill inferiority in them while slave owners and their families maintained superiority status. Owners were told to instill fear, distrust, and envy between them. Pitch the man against the woman and the light skinned black against the dark skinned black.

They were to create a dependency status toward the owners and a system that would be self-generating for thousands of years. The owners were to break their natural ability to care for themselves; cause them to be a dependent, not an independent people; reduce them from their natural state so they will only be productive for them. It was called, "The Making of a Slave."

Is it possible that The Willie Lynch indoctrination system was actually a curse that lasted the three hundred years as he predicted?

Did it cause this people to be dependent, needing man or government assistance, feeling inferior, fearful, unable to trust each other, and unable to really work together, overcome obstacles and build extraordinary businesses and projects?

Is there still a prejudice between light skin blacks and dark skin blacks, as Willie Lynch plotted and caused to occur between slaves? Does the division between the black man and women erected during slavery still exist today? Its purpose was to eliminate the black man from his family and use him as a stud, thus making his wife and family vulnerable to the master's rule. Then fearfully the black woman would train her children to submit and obey the master no matter what.

Has the Willie Lynch indoctrination system of 1712 been fulfilled in the black race in this country? Can we readily see its manifestation today in our cities and neighborhoods?

Well, I believe it was a curse but that curse can be broken. The Bible says in Proverbs 26:2 a cure without a cause will not alight. In other words there must be a reason or causes that allow the curse to be effective.

Actually we can trace curses of the black man from Africa of witchcraft, idolatry, selling and betraying blacks into slavery. These alone would create a landing ground for the Lynch decrees to release additional cures that are seen today in society.

The Lynch indoctrination was decreed in 1712 and 2012 marks the 300th year. It's time to take a stand and BREAK this plot and decree. Jesus Christ paid the price of freedom on the cross of Calvary. Why allow the system of elimination propagated by Margaret Sanger or Willie Lynch to extinguish the black family and community any longer?

Aborting the next generation is self-imposed genocide, and it is aligned with the plot of annihilation. It's time for a new paradigm and a new perspective of abundant life not elimination of it.

Why? Because that system certainly could not have been the purpose God ordained for the black man—to be deemed inferior and a subordinate race of people, suffering prejudice, slavery, discrimination, beatings, and stripped of their natural nature to care for themselves, all attributing to "death by abortion," because of skin color, a color and distinction that Almighty God gave him.

Originally, who was the black man in our Maker's heart before the foundation of the earth? Every ethnic group was assigned a purpose and destiny in the earth. What was the black man's? What did the Lord envision in His heart as a destiny for this people?

For years it was said that he was cursed because of the sin committed against Noah after the flood. After reading the Genesis account, however, we see that Noah cursed Ham's son Canaan and not Ham. If Ham had been cursed, that would have included all of his four children.

Since only Canaan was cursed, Cush, Put, and Mizraim, who were Ham's other black children, were not. Thus, it was Canaan's tribes that were cursed and Bible history proves that to be true with God's order to eliminate them from the promise land. (The Amalekites, Hittites, Perizzites, Hivites, and Ammonites).

Would a loving God create a people then purposely exterminate them at every opportunity, raping, killing, hanging, slavery and now *genocidal abortion*? God is love, and that is not love! It's hate!

Oh my! I got it! My "aha" moment! My paradigm shift! This assignment didn't originate with man. This struggle is not with flesh and blood. It's an assignment from hell. It's to cancel God's purpose for a people and ultimately God's plan for earth through this people.

Of course every ethnic group has an assignment and their problems on earth. So in no way am I saying only black people were mistreated. We are addressing, however, the genocide in the black family. It's apparent that the abortion numbers and the crisis in the black family, unfortunately, surpass other ethnicities.

Let's, therefore, go back to Abraham and the beginning. He is the father of the faith, but could he be father of many in the black race as well? The answer is yes! Abraham had three wives. After Sarah's death, he married Keturah, a Cushite, who bore him six children. They were Zimran, Jokshan, Medan, Midian, Ishbak, and Shuah in all, actually composing six nations resulting from this union, a fulfillment of God saying, "Abraham would be the father of many nations."

The genealogy of Keturah is not listed in the Bible. So we must trace her lineage through the names of her descendants. Genesis 25:3 states, "And Jokshan begat Sheba and Dedan and the sons of Dedan were Asshurim and Letushim and Leummim."

Now don't get lost. Genealogies can be tricky, but if you look closely you can see the generations as they line up. Jokshan had two sons and then his son Dedan had three sons—got it?

Jokshan was Abraham's and Keturah's second son, so their grandsons were Sheba and Dedan, who are listed in Genesis 10 as Cushites, who were black people.

Remember, all nations came from one blood (Acts 17). After the flood, Noah's three sons composed three people groups or races in the world: Shem the Jewish race, Japheth the Caucasian race, and Ham the black race. God blessed them and told them to multiply and replenish the earth.

We, therefore, can concur since Keturah's two grandsons are listed as Curshites, under Ham's lineage. Abraham's third wife was a black Cushite woman. Now that fact helps us see a powerful link of black lineage, but that's just the beginning.

God is faithful and He looks down through the generations to find a person with whom He can fulfill the purpose He has for a people, the destiny that was written in the books before the foundation of the earth.

In the book of Exodus we find a man named Jethro, who was called the Priest of Midian, positioned in the desert waiting for God's prophet to flee from Egypt for his safety.

Does that name Midian sound familiar? It should. It was the name of Abraham and Keturah's son. Keturah was Abraham's, third wife and a Cushite. Their heir is now chosen to mentor Moses, God's law giver and prophet, who would deliver Israel from Egypt. Moses had to be taken out of Egypt so God could reveal Himself to him. He had to unlearn forty years of Egyptian influence and be introduced to the covenant God of Abraham, Isaac, and Jacob.

Who better would instill the knowledge and counsel than a descendent of Abraham who still kept the faith and obeyed the commands of Abraham concerning Almighty God. Genesis 18:19 shares how Abraham commanded his children and household after him to keep the ways of the Lord.

Upon meeting Jethro, Moses gained favor and was granted permission to marry Zipporah, who was Jethro's daughter. This later caused a problem with Moses' siblings, Marian and Aaron, because she was an Ethiopian woman, (Numbers 12:1). It also points out the fact of Jethro's natural race. Ethiopian is another word for black. Ethiopian referred to dark skinned people of African descent or Negro.

Jethro is described as a priest in Exodus 18:12 that reads, "And Jethro, Moses father-in-law, brought a burnt offering and sacrifices to God and Aaron and all the elders of Israel, came and joined him in a sacrificial meal in God's presence". [NLT] They gave thanks to the Lord for the Egyptian victory. Notice that Jethro took the precedence in the priestly office rather than Aaron; no doubt because he was operating under the Abrahamic covenant based on an intimate faith relationship with God given prior to the Mosaic covenant, which had not yet, been given at Mount Sinai.

He soon saw Moses ministering to the multitude and counseled him on how to share the task of governing the people, an excellent management principle still used today. He was to divide the people into groups, choose capable men as judges to settle matters and bring important matters to Moses.

Apparently, during the wilderness journey, Jethro returned home, but left his son Hobab with Moses. Numbers 10 tells us that Hobab later also decided to return home, but Moses asked Hobab to journey with Israel to Canaan. At first, Hobab declined, desiring to see his kindred. However, Moses pleaded and prevailed when he said, "leave us not, I pray thee, forasmuch as you know how we are to camp in the wilderness and you will be our eyes. If you say yes and go with us, whatever goodness the Lord shall do unto us, *the same* will we do unto you," (Numbers 10:29–32).

Moses offered his Midianite brother-in-law the opportunity to reconnect with his Abrahamic inheritance. *Hobab was God's generational link to the original purpose of black people in the heart of God before the foundation of the world!* Hobab agrees and becomes *the eyes*, to Israel, and Joshua keeps the covenant made with these Kenite or Midianite peoples when they arrive in Canaan.[7]

Judges 1:16 says, "And the children of the Kenite, Moses' father-in-law, Jethro, went up out of the city of palm trees with the children of Judah into the wilderness of Judah, which lies in the south of Arad; and they went and dwelt among the people."

Did you get that? Black people were in the promise land, the land flowing with milk and honey. Would they now share in the inheritance with Judah?

Yes, Joshua kept the covenant Moses made with Hobab. It was in fulfillment of God's covenant with Abraham that he would be the father of many nations. Midian, the black son of Abraham and his third wife Keturah, who was also Jethro's heir, gained their inheritance along with the tribe of Judah. [8]

This is the key that unlocks the mystery. The God ordained purpose of black people as natural and spiritual heirs of Abraham. They are to inherit along with the tribe of Judah as worshippers and warriors, as well as, to serve as seers, prophetic seers in the kingdom. Moses told Hobab, *"You will be our eyes as we travel through the land."* Think of that: leaders, worshippers, and warriors!

Actually, you can identify much of this in the natural. Remember Motown? Or have you heard gospel singing or spirituals like "Swing Low, Sweet Chariot"? What about jazz, the blues, reggae, rap, and countless other styles? There is a natural sound of music that echoes from black people that is God ordained!

The warrior gifting, perverted now, because of years of mistreatment and fatherlessness, often manifests today as warriors of crime in our city streets. It's time to arise and reclaim that gifting as warriors for the Kingdom of God, destroying every stronghold and walking in Kingdom dominion, activating their ordained inheritance to influence the earth and be aligned with the one new man purposed by almighty God.

Unfortunately, there has been one diabolical strategy after another to eliminate black people and prevent them from occupying their leadership role in the world. Most attempts were external, but this plan of abortion has caused them to implode from within and eliminate the next generation.

Through government subsidy and legal blindness, Roe vs. Wade has led to an African-American genocide. Abortion disproportionately affects the African-American community more than any other ethnic group in America. Black women are four times more likely to have an abortion than white women.

Earlier we shared that 56 million babies have been aborted in the United States since 1973 and more than 16 million of them are black babies. That's 36.2 percent of all abortions in the United States. Human lives, devalued, cheapened, stolen by abortion.

This genocidal plan was birthed in the depths of hell, stoked by Willie Lynch, Margaret Sanger, institutional racism, and greed, then married to *Roe vs. Wade* and covered in legal blindness.

Enough is enough! It happened, its history, tell the story, but now is the time to say *NEVER* again! We are the ones who have lived to tell the story. We must say *NEVER* again... *WE MUST ARISE!*

I believe there is a parallel to the plight of the black man and Job. The story of Job, a righteous man in the Bible, was also tormented and suffered much by Satan. His property, livestock, children, and health were all destroyed, but he refused to curse God. He said there is a witness for me in heaven and I know my Redeemer lives! He kept his integrity. However, Job's friends accused him of sinning, but eventually God rebuked them and accused them of misrepresenting Him in the situation.

There was no answer given as to why Job suffered. As so often, the righteous do suffer wrong, and go without knowing the reason. However, like Job, there is a redeemer in heaven, and if you submit yourself to Him, Yahweh, the all-knowing and loving God, will bring restoration and redemption in His time.

I believe this for the black man as well, who cried out to God in the cotton fields and Underground Railroad routes, as they believed God for freedom even in the midst of suffering.

Job's friends were required to take a sacrificial offering of repentance to him and God said that Job would pray for them, at which time, the Lord would either accept Job's prayer or they would receive the punishment they deserved for their disgraceful behavior. They took their offering of repentance to Job, who prayed; God forgave them and restored double to Job of everything he had lost.

Think about it. Why did the Lord require Job's friends to go to him for prayer? Why take a burnt offering, and what did Job pray? I wonder what was in Job's prayer that caused God to restore double of everything he had lost. DOUBLE? Yes, twice as much as he had before!

What words are expressed in a prayer that returns double for your trouble? Was it only the words or was it the matter of the heart?

I believe Job forgave, and his friends repented with sincerity of heart. Both acts released a sacrificial fragrance before the Lord, a fragrance that pleased the Lord and bought restoration of everything lost.

There is a similar story of Corrie ten Boom that is familiar to many because of the film and her autobiography, *The Hiding Place*.

It tells of her life during World War II and Nazi occupation of the Netherlands. She and her family owned a watch shop and had cared for Jewish people for over one hundred years. They refused to ignore the atrocities being performed against their neighbors and opened their home as a hiding place for Jews seeking refuge.

The ten Booms proved they could be trusted, and their home became a sanctuary for hunted Jews. The family was betrayed, however, by a fellow Dutchman. They were arrested and sent to Ravensbruck, a Nazi death camp where conditions were appalling. There were long hours of forced labor, rat infested unheated barracks, malnutrition, disease, and physical abuse.

Corrie and her sister Betsey were able to reach out in love to the ravaged women around them and give them encouragement to trust God. Betsey died in prison on Christmas day in 1944. By a miracle Corrie was released soon afterwards through a clerical error. The rest of the women in her age group were exterminated a week later.

Corrie traveled to sixty-four countries before her death in 1983. She inspired millions of people with God's message of mercy, love, and forgiveness. On one occasion, while speaking in Germany about the power of forgiveness, she came face to face with one of the prison guards from Ravensbruck. This man had been one of the cruelest and most brutal guards from the death camp. The image of his face was deeply embedded into Corrie's horrific memories. As he stretched out his hand, with tears in his eyes, Corrie paused as her mind traced the painful past. Then slowly but deliberately gave him the forgiveness his soul longed for. Yes, she forgave Him!

To my surprise, as I read the above account, (written by Randy Bixby in his book *History Making Journeys of Faith and Character*, Volume 1) tears and a cry of remorseful rage arose in my heart. I could see the Nazi guard reaching out his hand to Corrie in my mind's eye. All of a sudden, however, I saw instead the whipping posts and heard the lashes that my ancestors endured.

I heard the degrading and debasing terms of racial horror. The many brutal hours in the cotton and sugar cane fields or those cutting lumber. The raping, hangings, and of all the inferior dehumanizing treatments they had to endure. Also included years of enslavement, rejection and humiliation, mentally and emotionally, being considered as outcasts and mere property.

Most of all the loss of identity and personhood that was denied by the Supreme Court in the Dred Scott Case of 1857 and the Plessey vs. Ferguson case in 1896 said, Black people were an inferior and subordinate class of people. Wow! Inferior, subordinate, words that wound a person's soul!

Then, all of a sudden I was overshadowed with the deep warm presence of God's love. It enveloped me and something broke inside of me. I stopped crying, and the rage, despair, and hurt slowly subsided. It was over. I sensed a deep heart of forgiveness, and a peace flooded my soul. I didn't experience the trauma Corrie or my ancestors endured, yet I did understand more the power of forgiveness. Thank you Lord for freedom. Thank you for the cross of Jesus!

It was my "aha" moment! I too forgave! Oh, it wasn't the first time. I had dealt with the issue before, but this time it touched my core being! I understood that for both Job and Corrie, it was forgiveness and the matter of the heart.

They forgave their persecutors. Forgiveness means to give up resentment against or the desire to punish; to stop being angry with; pardon. To give up all claim to punish or exact penalty for an offense; overlook. To cancel or remit a debt and to absolve.

Our greatest need was also forgiveness, so God sent us a Savior, Jesus Christ. Therefore, we must forgive so that the Father can forgive us our trespasses (Matthew 6).

It's interesting that Job, regardless of his suffering, never accused God. He had a deeper revelation of God's grace and sustaining providential care. He said, "I heard of you only by the hearing of the ear, but now my spiritual eye seeth you" (Job 42:5).

Job had an understanding of the Almighty God's love, rule, and might in the universe and bowed in reverence. "I know that you can do all things and that no thought, no purpose of yours, can be restrained or thwarted," Job said as he repented to God for questioning His headship. There was humility in Job that, I believe, touched the heart of God. It was the root the Lord wanted to preserve and show Satan there was a people who would love and be obedient to Him no matter what the circumstances. God loves to show off His kids!

That's the key if by faith we can see the greatness of God and His profound love. We will know nothing is impossible for Him.

Job's friends, however, had misrepresented God's character and misjudged his anointed servant Job. So they were required to make restitution or suffer the result of their deeds. They complied. Then the Lord blessed the latter days of Job more than his beginning. He had seven sons and three beautiful daughters. He lived 140 years and saw four generations of his sons.

God is not a respecter of persons. There must be an appointed time for healing the wounded root in black America and decreeing honor to an identity that was stolen, honor for a people upon whose backs this nation was built. There is an unpaid debt, and I believe the God of restoration will bring redemption to Black America as He did to Job.

Righteousness and justice is the foundation of the throne of God. Jesus came to earth to fulfill God's righteous justice and restore all things to its original purpose.

Hebrew 1:8–9 says, "Your throne, O God, will last forever and ever; a scepter of justice will be the scepter of your kingdom. You have loved righteousness and hated wickedness."

In Matthew 12:20, He says, "A bruised reed He will not break, and a smoldering (dimly burning) wick He will not quench, till He brings justice *and* a just cause to victory [Amp].

I believe that this injustice is one of the reasons why each time the Liberty Bell was rung it cracked. Perhaps it was a prophetic sign and testimony that America has a debt of injustice yet to be reconciled.

There needs to be true acknowledgment and reconciliation. True reconciliation only comes with redemption of that which was stolen. America's ground cries out with the slain blood of those taken until righteousness and justice prevails.

Then it will be time to arise and rebuild the ruins of the black family, cherish the foundation of many generations to come, and shift the present paradigm decreeing legally blind **no more!**

Chapter 7

RAISING THE STANDARD:

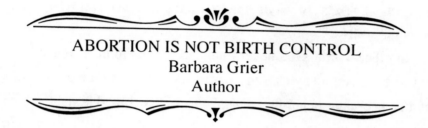

ABORTION IS NOT BIRTH CONTROL
Barbara Grier
Author

I am sympathetic to women who are not prepared to be pregnant for one reason or another. If that is the case, then we must deal with the real issue: Sex! That's how you become pregnant, right? It appears as though many in America today enjoy the benefits of sex without assuming the responsibility of the outcome. Or perhaps the main issue is that we no longer understand the original purpose of sex.

In the book, *The True Value of a Woman*, by Bishop Larry Jackson, he states that sex is primarily made for the woman, not the man. Therefore, it is meant to draw the man into a committed relationship for life. Like Jesus, he is to give up his life for his bride, total commitment.

However, today sex is being taught from a wrong focal point. When sex is centered on the needs of a man, it is cut and dry, but when centered on a woman, the experience is tied to her heart promoting

God's principle of leaving and cleaving. Proverbs 18:22 says "He who finds a wife finds a good thing and obtains favor of the Lord."

While attending the True Value Conference, in paraphrasing what Bishop Larry Jackson said, a man who gets the goods up front becomes a hunter and doesn't go into the cleaving mode. Women become devalued and are mere merchandise, and many women wonder why there is no proposal of marriage. I'm giving him everything. That's right, so why get married; the chase is over. The trophy is on the wall!

In other words, God never intended for sex to be a freebee. It's not to be given away as a toy or for recreation. When a woman's hymen is broken in her first sexual experience, blood is shed, which represents a covenant. God takes that seriously. A soul tie between the two people is now formed. Unfortunately, today sex has lost its value and has thus devalued women. Women are now sexual objects, and sexualizing in our society begins early even for our young girls.

The media has set the example for relationships and glamorized sexual behavior that eliminates the sacredness of sex and marriage. Sensuous, revealing clothes seem to be the choice today, even for many women in the church. Not even acknowledging that their attire has the ability to ignite a sexual response in the viewer and causing them to sin by visualizing what's under the clothes.

1 Thessalonians 4:6 says that no man should go beyond and defraud his brother in any manner. *Defraud* means to be deprived of something by deception. Revealing sensuous clothing is deceptive because it shows something that the viewer is cheated out of having. It's like holding out a carrot then saying, oops, you can't have this, big boy! That defrauds the viewer.

Media and celebrity sexual role models are being adopted by today's women at a rapid pace, thus, I believe, contributing to opening the door for sex trafficking, kidnappings, and, sex crimes ignited by unbridled sexual appetites fueled in society, not to mention the growing numbers of sexually transmitted diseases, which increase at nineteen million new cases each year. Almost half of them are among youth aged fifteen to twenty-four years of age. [1] We are facing a silent crisis in our nation because of sexual diseases.

Cheryl Wetzstein, of the *Washington Times*, exposed an existing crisis in her article, "Sounding the Alarm on Gonorrhea" (April 27, 2010). Wetzstein quotes William Smith, the head of the National Coalition of STD Directors, about a strain of gonorrhea and how it could affect every part of America. In his words, "We are on the verge of a highly untreatable outbreak of the disease." It is dangerous because it is almost completely resistant to antibiotics. According to the account, even the Centers for Disease Control have just a single class of antibiotics left to treat. Cases reported in 2013 of 333,004 by CDC reveal a needed reduction in cases.

Nevertheless, breaking God's commandments can release curses like this disease into society. The gift of sex was created with great value because it creates another life in the image of God. Sex was created to be precious, passionate, powerful, a present, pure, and private to be protected in marriage.

Sex was made for marriage, and marriage was made for love. God purposed that the gift of sex would be protected in a committed marriage between a man and a woman. Together they would become one flesh before Him.

One of my favorite biblical characters is Joseph. He is an excellent example of someone who passed the sexual purity test.

In the book, *From Dream to Destiny*, by Robert Morris, he says that

> Our popular culture may declare that sexual morality has nothing to do with character, but God begs to differ: Sexual morality has everything to do with character and if we are going to walk in the destiny God ordained, we must understand what He says about sexual purity. (Luke 16:10, "If we are unfaithful in little things we will be unfaithful in much"

If a person is immoral in one area of his life, he will also be immoral in another area, which includes sex. The Bible says to flee fornication and adultery.

David was an example of being sexually immoral. He committed adultery with Bathsheba, and then he lied and committed murder. Usually other acts are needed to cover up a sin. This was a stain on David's character and consequences followed.

However, Joseph passed the test. He had learned to steward his own appetites. Genesis 39 tells us how Potiphar's wife begged him daily to sleep with her. Finally, catching him alone in the house, she tried to seduce him; but Joseph ran and left his coat. He said, "How can I do such a great wickedness against God?" He realized he was not only sinning against his master, but also God.

We are all sexual beings, and God created sex for us to enjoy with our spouse. But the gift has the responsibility of stewardship attached to it. That understanding and commitment seems to be what is missing in our society today. Abstinence and discipline until marriage is the answer, and it still works. Remember abortion is not birth control.

God has ordained that sex is the bond that seals a marriage between one man and one woman in a lifetime commitment. With God, a three-way cord is not easily broken.

Our Founding Fathers believed that religion and morality were inseparable for good government and they were necessary for national success. President John Adams said, "Our constitution was made only for a moral and religious people. It is wholly inadequate to the government of any other."

The original intent of the constitution by the founding fathers was that a self-governing nation was only built upon self-governing individuals who adhered to morals and religious principles. [2]

One example of those principles today would be the sanctity of life in the womb. That was the original intent of our founding fathers. They wrote in the Declaration of Independence that all men were created equal, they are endowed by their creator with certain unalienable rights that among these are *life*, liberty, and the pursuit of happiness.

My friend, sex makes babies, babies that are precious, valuable, and made in the image of almighty God. They have a destiny and purpose in the earth. Abortion terminates that destiny. It is not birth control; it is murder.

Chapter 8

BABY MAKER CRADLE SHAPER

They overcame Him by the blood of the lamb and by the
word of their testimony and they loved not their lives
unto death. – Revelations 12:11 KJV

The hand that rocks the cradle shapes the nation was a cliché years ago. Although the saying is outdated, the concept still holds true. Women whose womb is the door to the universe have also been given the divine ability to shape a nation, shape it as she nurtures and molds the life of each child delivered into her care.

This assignment, however, because of its divine importance, has attracted the attention of the evil one who is determined to hinder and or destroy the mission. Legal blindness is a major tool. Women, thus, have been the object of much wounding and harm. Genesis 3 describes the enmity between the serpent and the woman that occurred in the garden in Eden. That enmity still exists today.

Women have been the subject of much injustice and wounding because Satan hates women. Not only was the birth of Christ brought through a woman, but every other potential follower of Jesus comes through the door of a woman and is touched one way or another by her life.

Because of this attack, the enemy has stolen much from women, including inheritances, property, identity, social status, businesses, employment, and the one attack with the greatest impact on society is abortion.

Abortion robs women of their God-ordained influence on society from the womb as well as, their legacy. The womb was not to be a tomb but an entrance to *life* on earth. The theory that abortion is a part of a woman's health is a carefully plotted deception fueled by greed, selfishness, and ignorance of the facts. It is the root of legal blindness.

The true facts and results of abortions are best told by women who themselves have suffered the trauma and wound in one form or another. I have, therefore, included in this chapter the voices of women and men who share their stories. Listen with your heart and see it through their eyes.

These testimonies are not to frighten you but to reveal the truth. It is the truth that set you free.

Let's begin with Lynne's story. As a catharsis, she wrote her testimony to warn other women of the emotional and spiritual consequences of abortion.

Here are her words:

As a young girl, I had been firmly committed to virginity until marriage. A number of my sisters had gotten pregnant before marriage. I saw their struggles and I was determined to remain a virgin. However, at the age of 20, my father was in jail with a 19 month sentence and our family lives in shambles. I didn't care anymore about saving myself for marriage. So I had my first sexual encounter and after several other events, I found myself pregnant.

I couldn't believe that something as unpleasant as my first sexual experience could get me pregnant. It just wasn't fair. However, it was my junior year in college and time to go home for Christmas break. When I arrived home, I went to a neighborhood clinic to learn I was over four months pregnant, Oh no! This was going to cause a major upset to the plans for my life. After talking to my mother and her pleading with me not to have an abortion, I proceeded to abort anyway. I can still hear my mother weeping as she said, "We don't kill our children in this family!" I should have listened!

I remember it was in 1973 when I left home and went to a hospital in New York. I was shocked to see so many women there. I registered, paid my money and went into the examination room. The doctor told me I was so far along that labor had to be induced and he was going to inject saline into my uterus. That caused a chemical imbalance which is contrary to life, causing the child to be born dead with chemical burns all over its body.

I was released later that day, physically, still bleeding and my body trying to repair itself. Spiritually, I was dead; but emotionally, I felt relieved, believing it was all over. Unfortunately, it was not!

During the weeks that followed, voices of guilt, remorse, and self-justification bombarded me. It was constant. I sought out companionship so I wouldn't hear the voices. I played music. I was so depressed that all I wanted to do was cry.

The act of abortion caused wounds in my emotions, tears and rips in my personality. I had done something that my conscience would not tolerate and I was constantly in torment because I had committed murder. I had opened myself up to a murderous spirit. I was guilty, depressed and had suicidal thoughts. I seldom slept.

I began drinking a lot of alcohol. I felt hopeless, worthless and wanted to die. I knew I would kill myself if I stayed in my apartment during spring break, so I went back home to Chicago. I had to face my mother, but it didn't matter by then. My mother, however, welcomed me with open arms and never spoke of the issue.

While at home, the Lord revealed His salvation to Lynn. His love and the healing process began in her life. It was a new beginning. It took time but faithfully He restored her fragmented soul. She is whole and free today. To God be the glory.

You can read Lynne's complete story in her book *Destinies Denied*. [1]

Here is Jerry's story:

> My name is Jerry and I am a post abortion father. Public opinion would suggest that men are not supposed to be affected by abortion. That is wrong! I can bear witness to the fact that men are actually very affected by their abortion involvement.
>
> Thirty five years ago, I had a relationship with a girl that ended in abortion. It actually seemed convenient at the time and was kept a secret. What I didn't realize then was how this would affect me for the next 30 plus years of my life. Without my even realizing it, the guilt of what I had been part of created anxiousness, anxiety and an anger hidden deep inside of me that I just could not understand. My father and I were very close and when he died of brain cancer a few years ago, my anger finally boiled over. My wife insisted that I get help. Through my counseling for anger, my experience with abortion finally came to the surface. I was connected with a post abortion counselor at a local pregnancy center. As I worked through a study called "Healing a Fathers Heart," I realized how deeply this spirit of abortion had gripped my life. It had deeply affected my thoughts and it had adversely affected relationships with family and others. It had kept me distant from my God. I was so

angry at those responsible for my daughter's death that I really wanted to hurt them.

When I finally forgave those responsible for killing my little girl, there was a huge weight lifted off of me. The power of forgiveness was like nothing I have ever experienced in my life. It was miraculous, life changing and brought me tremendous freedom. I was free of the anxiety, the anger and the anxiousness that had been with me for so many years. Relationships with family and others that had been difficult for years suddenly changed. I feel closer to God then I had ever felt in my life. I now have a joy in living that I have never experienced before.

I will probably never stop grieving for my daughter, but I can tell you that I no longer carry the guilt and shame of what I have done. I have been forgiven and Praise the Lord.

This is Angela's story as a participant in the abortion industry. Angela was a nurse at a hospital in Southwest Detroit.

I was often asked to assist in abortions and we did many per day. My job was to take the product of conception and place all the pieces on the table. We kept a bucket of water there and to make us feel better, (I now believe) we would sprinkle the body parts with water. We would then say, "In the name of the Father, Son and Holy Ghost we baptize you!"

We were also to make sure that all of the body parts from the child were accounted for, two arms, legs, feet, etc. No body parts were to be left in the woman's body.

At that time, I felt that the issue was between the woman and her doctor. I must have witnessed hundreds of abortions. It was just a ritual to me. I hardened my heart to the reality that it was a life that was being terminated.

While in Maryland, I witnessed the abortion of a fully formed baby that was placed in a basin, covered with a towel and allowed to slowly die. It was a Caesarian section and six months old. It was breathing, kicking and alive. Now, that broke my heart and it was hard to watch, but I made myself believe it was not my business. It was a game changer without realizing it at the time. Slowly, I began to change and gradually God touched my heart to acknowledge Him and to know that life began at conception. Wow! Up until that time I believed what I was told. However, now the light came on, paradigms shift.

I realized then, that I had been committing murder and I asked God to forgive me. I am still a nurse, but

refuse now to participate in abortions. When I find
myself in that situation I immediately say, "Not me,
I'm out of here." The industry often assumes you'll
comply, but not me anymore.

Life is precious and I am willing to even lose my
job if need be. I will not participate in murder. I've
been set free.

That was Angela's "aha" moment, and I could feel her resolve as
she shared her testimony with me.

Unfortunately, the list of women utilizing abortion centers is long
and growing to exercise their "choice," only to leave in a body bag
or ambulance. Regrettably, not every woman survives the wounding
of an abortion.

You must hear Tamie and Tonya's stories. I pray their choice will
give you an understanding of the real risks in abortions.

Tamie Russell was just fifteen years old, when she went to the
Woman's Care of Southfield, Michigan Abortion Center on January
7, 2004. She wanted to terminate a six-month pregnancy and, her
boyfriend's sister drove her to the facility to obtain an abortion. She
had no parental consent or judicial bypass as required by state law.

The next day she returned to the facility complaining of bleeding
heavily. Before she could get to a hospital, she died of uterine infarc-
tion due to post-secondary trimester abortion resulting in a blockage
in her uterine blood vessel, ultimately leading to a sepsis infection.
According to the medical examiner, "It is suspected that the abortion drug RU-486 CAUSED THE FATAL INFECTION THAT
CLAIMED HER LIFE."

According to WJBK Fox News in Detroit, Russell's relatives say on January 7th, she confessed to being pregnant with her twenty-four-year-old boyfriend's child and that his sister had driven her to the Woman Care of Southfield facility to obtain an abortion.

"It won't bring her back, but I want them to pay," Nicola Powell, Russell's cousin, told Fox News. "Then they won't do nobody else's baby like that."[2]

Another young life destroyed because someone in that scenario did not value life in the womb. I feel so compelled to share these outcomes of botched abortions. Who else will tell you the real truth?

Here is Tonya Reaves' story:

A copy of Tonya Reaves' autopsy report says that the twenty-four-year-old woman died from three major complications during an abortion at a Chicago area Planned Parenthood abortion clinic on July 20, 2012.

I want you to hear this actuate account. Please allow the blinders to come off.

Troy Newman, the head of Operation Rescue and Pro-Life Nation, told Life News he is saddened by Reaves' death.

Operation Rescue obtained the full autopsy results and said they indicated that Reaves' injuries were survivable if she had received proper emergency care in a timely manner. It was a botched abortion!

> Abortion deaths like this are completely avoidable. When a woman bleeds to death after an abortion, it is usually an indication of error on the part of the abortionist coupled with a delay in calling for emergency assistance. Planned Parenthood should be held accountable, said Troy Newman. Our heartfelt

prayers go out to the victim's family at this time of tragic loss. [3]

Tonya was a healthy woman who was approximately 16 weeks pregnant at the time of her abortion, and was well into her second trimester.

As I share these accounts I can picture billboard pictures of these women lining our nation's highways, describing the needless deaths they suffered by abortion.

Botched abortions are resulting from legal blindness to the value of life in the womb.

The next account sounds like it's a preview of a horror movie, but it's not.

It is called the House of Horrors because it is the brutal account of Dr. Kermit Gosnell who in 2011 was charged with eight counts of murder and a host of other offenses. It was a nightmare of abortions uncovered in Pennsylvania. Dr. Gosnell was charged with gross medical malpractice in treatment of patients at his clinics, as well as several lesser offenses.

The murder charges related to a patient who died while under his care and seven newborns said to have been killed after being born alive during attempted abortions. In May 2013, he was convicted on three of the murder charges. After his conviction, Gosnell waived his right of appeal in exchange for an agreement not to seek the death penalty. He was sentenced instead to life in prison without the possibility of parole.

I will spare you all the morbid details, only to say the court document describes his clinic as unbearably despicable. The Drug Enforcement Administration (DEA) investigating team when describing to the Grand Jury the conditions of the clinic during the 2010 raid reported it was "filthy, unsanitary, very outdated, horrendous, and by far, the worst that these experienced investigators had ever encountered."

Semi-conscious women scheduled for abortions were moaning in the waiting room. Many had been sedated by unlicensed staff long before Gosnell arrived at the clinic. Many of the medications in inventory were past their expiration dates. "Surgical procedure rooms were filthy and unsanitary... resembling a bad gas station restroom."

Instruments were not sterile. Equipment was rusty and outdated. Oxygen equipment was covered with dust and had not been inspected. The same corroded suction tubing used for abortions was the only tubing available for oral airways if assistance for breathing was needed.

Fetal remains were haphazardly stored throughout the clinic—in bags, milk jugs, and orange juice cartons and even in cat food containers! [4]

Dr. Kermit Gosnell was a college graduate with a medical degree he received in 1966. It was reported that he spent four decades practicing medicine among the poor. In 1972, he opened up an abortion clinic, and he received referrals from the major abortion organizations in the nation.

A 1972 National Enquirer article said that Gosnell was a "respected man" in his community. He was not a back alley doctor as the abortion industry *now* proclaims after his fall from grace.

The point I'm making here is that this clinic illustrates the so-called woman's health care that is found in many of the abortion clinics in the nation and the uncaring physicians and unprofessional unlicensed staff. But this despicable clinic was sanctioned and a part of the Pennsylvania medical facilities.

However, abortions clinics are not monitored regularly as was the case with Gosnell and reportedly many others. So you take your life in your own hands, as many lamenting families report today.

Testimonies and life accounts tell the true stories. That was my purpose in sharing the sad and unfortunate events in the lives of those mentioned. I'm sure there are those who will claim their abortions had absolutely no side effects. So be it, but if these testimonies spared anyone remorse and pain, to God be the glory.

The choice of abortion can result in great complications.

Abortion is a risky choice.

It is important that you know the choice of abortion is very hazardous. Please understand that every medical procedure presents many surgical or medical risks.

Personally I always look at the side effects of every medication I am given, and that also goes for procedures. I have even cancelled some procedures and not taken medication after reading its possible negative effects. Call me chicken, but I don't like pain. Ouch!!

Therefore, let me advise you of the risk for abortion. Most clinics will not share the following information. So I feel it is my duty to inform all my sisters.

For abortion the related risks are nausea, heavy bleeding, infection, incomplete abortion—some fetal parts may not be properly removed, thus causing bleeding or infection, tearing of cervix—which can create complications in future pregnancies, searing of uterine lining—which can cause sterility, perforation of uterus, damage to internal organs, and death.

There is also a post-abortive emotional impact. It can occur days or years after the abortion. Some of the symptoms are eating disorders, relationship problems, guilt and depression, flashbacks of the abortion, suicidal thoughts, sexual dysfunction, and alcohol and drug abuse.

Effects on future pregnancies may mean higher risks of miscarriage for those who abort their first pregnancy. The link to *breast cancer* is higher for women who had an abortion before age eighteen or after thirty for women who have no children and have had one or more abortions. [5] Their risk is 50 percent higher than normal genetic risk. [6]

There are reports of women becoming sterile with perforated uterus's bowels ripped out and cervix torn among other injuries, as well as, discoveries of ectopic pregnancies resulting in loss of right and or left fallopian tubes.

Earlier this year there was a case before the United States Court of Appeals Eighth Circuit in the State of Arkansas representing both women wounded by abortion and abortion survivors. Its purpose was to supply the court with personal accounts of women who suffered physical and psychological injuries because of abortion, and one individual who survived multiple attempts by her parents to cause her abortion or miscarriage.

This Justice Foundation brief, led by lead council Allan E. Parker Jr. can be viewed for your inspection. [7]

Few know that many women are secretly tormented by the dark and painful secrets, thoughts of suicide, guilt, shame, nightmares, sleeplessness, and depression after an abortion.

Abortion is not a joke! Your life is on the line, so be well advised, not legally blind.

Chapter 9

WHAT'S YOUR PARADIGM?

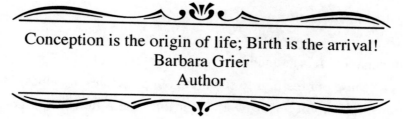

Conception is the origin of life; Birth is the arrival!
Barbara Grier
Author

When I began writing *Legally Blind*, I asked you to consider the information and examine your own paradigm, the lens through which you view the world. In so doing, you must allow your self-awareness to help you determine whether your paradigm is reality or principle based. Or is it a function of conditioning or conditions, as Steven R. Covey states in *The 7 Habits of Highly Effective People*?

Covey states there are several theories that suggest the nature of man causes him to operate in various ways. The first would be genetic and based on the DNA of your grandparents. Second would be the psyche, based on your parents. Last, you are the product of your environment. Something or someone in your environment is responsible for your character and tendencies.

I am impressed with, however, the theory by Victor Frankel. While imprisoned in the death camp of Nazi Germany, he discovered a fundamental principle about the nature of man. He was tortured and exposed to the most inhumane treatment possible, but one human freedom could not be taken from him, the power to choose how he would respond. He could decide how all of this was going to affect him. Between what happened to him, the stimulus, and his response to it, was the freedom or power to choose his response. That is called the proactive model. [1]

It means you, as a human being, are responsible for your life and your behavior. It is a function of your decisions, not your conditions. We can cause our feelings to submit to our principles or values. That is our responsibility. However, if our lives are a function of conditioning and conditions, it's because we have by conscious decision or by default chosen to empower those things to control us. Thus, we become reactive. These are people who are affected by their physical environment. If, for example, it's snowing, they become house bound. Reactive people are driven by feelings, circumstances, conditions, and environment.

On the contrary, proactive people are driven by carefully thought about internalized values and principles. Their decisions are value and principle-based choices no matter the stimuli or situation.

Nelson Mandela spent twenty-seven years in a South African prison. When he was released, he did not function in retaliation mode. He instead, formed a government for all the people of South Africa. His testimony was that one day as he was working in the rock quarry, he realized the government had taken everything from him but one thing, and that was how his heart would respond. He chose to be proactive.

History tells us that he was known as one of the kindest, loving persons you could meet. People were amazed by his responses. His paradigm was proactive and based on principles of character.

Character principles are those that are universally unchangeable, regardless of religion or individual background. Principles like fairness, integrity, human dignity, excellence, service and growth are all common to mankind. They may be achieved differently, but there is universal awareness of them.

Remember, a paradigm is like a pair of glasses you wear that influences the way you see everything in life. It affects all your attitudes and behaviors.

After your examination, what do you believe is your paradigm? What eye glass perspective determines how you see the world and what **principles** make your decisions and determines your behavior?

In chapter one I shared why most women choose abortions. Observing the reasons, it was clear that most were based on conditions, environment, or personal preferences. Little or no consideration was given to the unborn child.

My premise for writing this book is that *Roe vs. Wade* has made Americans blind to the fact that the unborn child is alive and a person, regardless of its location.

Science has clearly given evidence that the unborn are a living, distinct, whole human being and abortion ends the life of a human being... a living, breathing person.

I heard John Paul Jackson, a prophet; say something earlier that really made sense. It dealt with the definitions of the words truth and facts. He indicated both are not the same.

There are really four views of truth. First, there is moralistic or cultural view based on habits and customs of ethnic or various groups. Second, there is the relative view that says "the means justifies the end," or this is true because of the circumstance right now. Third, there is the multiple level truth, or "this was true years ago, but, it is a new day now and no longer relevant." Last, there is the symbolic truth which says, "Well, Jesus is only a symbol of how things should be. He really didn't live. He didn't save the world."

With all these views, no wonder people say, it's just relative. Truth seems to evolve and follow popular opinion. But real truth is applicable no matter where, when, or with whom you find it. Real truth never changes. That's why the truth is only found in God. His word is true. His Spirit is called the Spirit of Truth.

Truth is more than facts because it has more than one level. For instance, when Abraham went to Egypt, he told Pharaoh that Sarah was his sister. That was a fact, but not the truth. She was really his wife, but he gave only a fact because he feared Pharaoh would kill him. Truth has a deeper level, which includes the motive behind the fact.

In Acts 16:16, the servant girl who followed Paul said, "these are the servants of the highest God." The truth was that she was establishing herself as a spiritual authority so when Paul left, the people would believe and follow her. That was the truth. The truth must be connected to the motive or is it just fact and not truth.

Looking at the case of *Roe vs. Wade*, the question arises, is it based on fact or truth? The Court issued its decision on January 23, 1973, with a 7 to 2 majority vote in favor of Roe. The Court's decision deemed abortion a *fundamental right* under the Due Process Clause of the Fourteenth Amendment of the United States Constitution.

In many cases, we hear them describe fundamental rights as those rights that pre-exist the foundation of the United States; in essence, an element of humanity, rather than a construct of government, often termed "God-given right," human rights," or "natural rights."

Here we see that a fundamental right is classified as a God-given right. I ask you, is this really truth? Where does God say that a woman has been given the fundamental right to abort her baby? Does that also include toddlers, which are babies as well? Also, if abortion is a right, that pre-existed the foundation of the United States, then why was it considered a crime in most of the United States for 200 years?

For instance, in Texas where the *Roe vs. Wade* trial occurred, the plaintiff came against the criminality of the abortions law. Abortion was considered a crime unless for rape, health of mother, etc. Think about it. Is abortion a natural right, a human right, a God-given right, or a right given by the government? Has the government now made a fact an absolute truth?

In Isaiah 59:14 the prophet declares that truth has fallen in the street. There is no justice, righteousness, or honesty. There is such deterioration in the land that there is no one to intervene for truth.

The Message Bible says it like this:

> Justice is beaten back, righteousness banished to the
> sidelines, truth staggers down the street. Honesty is
> nowhere to be found and good is missing in action.
> Anyone renouncing evil is beaten and robbed.

There is a famous poem by Martin Niemoller entitled: "First They Came." It says,

First they came for the Communist, but I wasn't a
Communist, so I didn't speak up. Then they came
for the Jews, but I wasn't a Jew, so I didn't speak up.
Then they came for the Trade Unionist, but I wasn't a
Trade Unionist, so I didn't speak up. Then they came
for the Catholics, but I wasn't a Catholic, so I didn't
speak up. Then they came for me and there was no
one left to speak for me"

When truth is fallen in the street and ignored, there will be no
real justice. Eventually, everyone will be affected and left to suffer
for their silence.

When abortion is accepted as truth and tolerated in order to be
politically correct, who will be left to speak for you when cloning,
euthanasia, or other fact-filled policies are introduced as law in
society? What will you say when that truth falls at your feet?

Jesus said, "I am the way, the truth and the life," (John 14:6),
and "Ye shall know the truth, and the truth shall make you free,"
(John 8:32).

Psalm 139:13–16 shares how God formed every person before
the womb. I love the Message Bible translation. Let's read how the
scripture is made easy to understand.

Oh yes, you shaped me first inside, then out; you
formed me in my mother's womb. I thank you, High
God—you're breathtaking! Body and soul, I am mar-
velously made! I worship in adoration—what a creation! You know me inside and out, you know every
bone in my body. You know exactly how I was made,

bit by bit, how I was sculpted from nothing into something. Like, an open book, You watched me grow from conception to birth; all the stages of my life were spread out before you. The days of my life all prepared, before I'd even lived one day.

God's word is truth. It is the same yesterday, today, and forever. It is not subject to culture, time, or symbolism because God is truth. That is His name, and that is His character. There is no need to look for a standard of measurement because He is the standard. That's why His word is truth, not just a fact.

Birth is not the origin of life; it is the arrival. Life begins at conception, and it is a precious, valuable gift from God with purpose.

The Lord told Jeremiah, "Before I formed you in the womb, I knew you and set you apart to be a Prophet to the nations."

The issue here is that the unborn is made in the likeness and image of God from conception, a truth not to be taken lightly.

Interestingly, we later learned that truth actually became an issue with Norma McCorvey. She was the Roe in the *Roe vs. Wade* case.

I have included her testimony. It highlights her life and the conflict few knew she encountered during the *Roe vs. Wade* case. It's an example of truth fallen in the street.

In 1970, Norma McCorvey, under the pseudonym "Jane Roe," filed a lawsuit challenging the Texas laws that criminalized abortion. The case eventually reached the United States Supreme Court as the now-famous *Roe vs. Wade*. "Roe," is described as a pregnant woman who, "wished to terminate her pregnancy by an abortion performed by a competent, licensed physician, under safe and clinical conditions."

As Norma McCorvey tells the true story, she describes herself "as having been relatively ignorant of the facts of her own case and claims that her attorneys simply used her for their own predetermined ends. They were looking for somebody, anybody, to use to further their own agenda. I was their most willing dupe." She had indeed become pregnant with her third child and sought to end her pregnancy, but she was not aware of all the implications of abortion or even what the term itself meant.

"Abortion, to me, meant going back to the condition of not being pregnant." She did not fully realize that this process would end a human life. She says that her attorney Sarah Weddington, rather than correcting her misconceptions, deliberately confused the issue; "For their part, my lawyers lied to me about the nature of abortion. Weddington convinced me, it's just a piece of tissue. You just missed your period."[2][3]

Another problem was that Norma claimed that her pregnancy was the result of a gang rape, in order to present a more sympathetic picture. As she has since admitted, this was totally untrue!

Norma also states that her actual involvement in the case was minimal. She signed the initial affidavit without even reading it and was never invited into court. Norma said, "I never testified! I was never present before any court on any level and I was never at any hearing on my case... I found out about the decision from the newspaper just like the rest of the country."

Norma never had an abortion! She gave her baby up for adoption!

In 1980, she became involved in the abortion movement, making public appearances in support of abortion. Around 1992, she began to work at abortion clinics. When Norma was working a clinic in Dallas in 1995, a pro-life group moved into the same building, leading to a series of dramatic encounters.

Over time, she became friends with many of them and began to have serious doubts about the morality of abortion.

She was particularly affected by her friendship with Emily Mackey, the seven-year-old daughter of one of the pro-lifers. She began to realize what abortion was doing to children. Abortion was no longer an abstract right. It had a face now, in a little girl named Emily. [4]

Eventually (due in large part to Emily's urging) she started going to church and began to reject her past involvement with the pro-abortion movement.

Since her conversion, she has dedicated herself to pro-life work, starting her own ministry, "Roe No More," in 1997 and continuing to speak out against abortion and for life. In 2003, she went to court in an attempt to overturn *Roe vs. Wade*. Her case was dismissed by the Fifth Circuit Appeals Court. However, one of the judges wrote a strong concurrence opinion critical of the *Roe vs. Wade* decision. Here is the statement from Judge Edith Jones:

> Finally, neonatal and medical science, summarized by McCorvey, now graphically portrays as science was unable to do 31 years ago, how a baby develops sensitivity to external stimuli and to pain much earlier than was then believed. If courts were to delve into the facts underlying Roe's balancing scheme with present day knowledge, they might conclude that the woman's "choice" is far more risky and less beneficial

and the child's sensitivity is far more advanced than
the Roe Court knew. [5]

Norma's testimony is an excellent example of a situation based
on facts not on the truth.

The companion case of *Doe vs. Dalton* is also an example of facts
manipulated to appear as truth. Sandra Cano, the Doe in this case did
not want an abortion nor did she have one. She was young and des-
perate and made to believe she was signing for a divorce. The link
to the entire transcript of Sandra's case is included in the endnotes
for your reference. [6]

I feel compelled also to include a recent testimony of a woman
whose testimony to the 8th circuit court in Arkansas explain how
abortion wounded her. It clearly illustrates the difference between a
fact and the truth.

Her name is Lisa:

> I was told it was a mass of tissue. I was NOT told that
> at the time of my abortion, all arteries are present,
> including the coronary vessels of the heart and that
> blood was fully circulating through these vessels to
> all body parts. I was NOT told that the "mass of tissue"
> had complete vocal chords and that the brain was fully
> formed and that the "mass of tissue" had organized
> muscles, could feel pain, suck its thumb, and had eye
> lids that protected its delicate optical nerve fibers.
>
> I was NOT told that the flutters I felt were actually
> kicks and movements of the "mass of tissue"... of

course, I did hear them say in the middle of the abortion "she is farther along than we thought" as I cried for them to stop... "It's too late, honey. You did the right thing. Now, you can go on with your life." I could hear the water running in the sink nearby. I then heard a big plop..."Did you just throw my baby in the trash?" I thought.... Then they shuffled me out the back way.

They told me I would forget about the "mass of tissue" and be able to go on with my life, but I was having nightmares every night. For many years, a day did not go by that I did not contemplate suicide. Guilt, sorrow, loss of dignity and deep shame are the most felt responses after an abortion. I experienced deep despair and lonely scars of regret." [7]

My friend, now that is truth, not just facts!

I believe *Roe vs. Wade* has caused people to have loss of acuity or keenness of vision regarding the unborn child, thus embracing a paradigm that sanctions a law that accepts murdering a child in the womb. Individual government subsidy for the largest abortion industry, Planned Parenthood actually grossed one half billion dollars in 2012. There is a national atmosphere for abortion to be a means of birth control and a paradigm in which people deny or reject the **truth** of the personhood of the unborn child.

Our heavenly Father has made all life a prerequisite. If you find that *Roe vs. Wade* has caused your paradigm to be distorted, I invite

115

you to put first things first. Position the sanctity and life of the unborn child first, reject abortion, and be legally blind no more.

Chapter 10

ABORTION INJURES FAMILIES

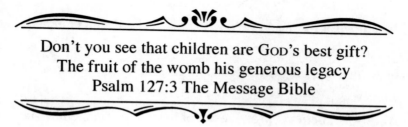

Don't you see that children are GOD's best gift?
The fruit of the womb his generous legacy
Psalm 127:3 The Message Bible

G od is a family man. Before the creation of Adam and his uniting with Eve, the Godhead—Father, Son and Holy Spirit—existed as a family. A family unit is what God desired to duplicate on earth.

Nevertheless, from Genesis to Revelation the Bible tells of Satan's continual efforts to be God. His focus was to adopt and make God's family his own. Deception, division, and rejection were some of the tools used to cause the family structure to splinter. In Malachi the Lord reveals the state of the family in the lasts days.

It is fragmented and needing restoration of the father's heart to the children, and theirs to their father. The prophet Malachi writes in 4:5–6:

Behold, I will send you Elijah the prophet before the coming of the great and dreadful day of the LORD:

And he shall turn the heart of the fathers to the children, and the heart of the children to their fathers, lest I come and smite the earth with a curse.

We are now in the last days and are experiencing an onslaught of attacks against the family. No doubt Satan's plan is to offset the Elijah spirit that would change the heart of mankind and heal the family unit. Our family units are indeed under attack.

It is time for those anointed with the fire, love, and compassion of Elijah to arise in this season. Arise in the Spirit of God with healing in His wings, restoring the breach and eliminating every curse against the family.

Abortion, I believe, is one result of the curses decreed in Malachi. The verse indicated that the heart of the fathers would return to their children OR a curse would result. A father's heart saturated with God's love would protect and cherish his child, not abort it.

Currently, we face a crisis of fatherlessness in America. According to the U.S. Census Bureau, (43%) twenty-four million children in America... live in biological father-absent homes. I believe this is a major factor to the abortion issue. [1]

Research shows when a child is raised in a father-absent home; he or she is affected in the following ways: greater risks of poverty, teen pregnancy, infant mortality, child abuse, high school dropout, behavior problems, drug usage, crime, and obesity. [2]

In the book *The Future War of the Church*, Chuck Pierce says "One of the ways Satan draws kids into lawlessness is through fatherlessness. Our young people must have fathers in the days ahead. My father died when I was sixteen. Since that time the Lord has always made certain I had a spiritual father in my life. I have always submitted to these father figures whom God brought into my life to help grow me into the destiny for which I was created."

So you may ask why the father is the key factor. One answer is that in Hebrew the definition and word for father is Aleph Bet, which means the strength of the house.

If the father is removed from the home, the family unit is in disrepair. God ordained that the father be the strength of the home. He bands the home together. Husband! [Hus-band].

Facts show that father's absence is an important factor in teen sexual activity, pregnancy, and abortion.

Statistics indicate being raised by a single mother raises the risk of teen pregnancy; in fact it is reported that a teen is seven times more likely to get pregnant in a father-absent home. [3]

In 2008 the Guttmacher Institute reported that "Eighteen percent of U.S. women obtaining abortions were teenagers; those aged 15–17 obtain 6% of all abortions, 18–19-year-olds obtain 11%, and teens younger than 15 obtain 0.4%." [4]

It appears the trend in the U.S. indicates about a quarter of all teenage pregnancies end in abortion. "Four in five (82 percent) teenage pregnancies are unintended, and two out of every five (37 percent) unintended teen pregnancies in 2006 ended in *abortion*." [5]

God's original plan for a family was to illustrate the love, wholeness, and unity existing in the triune God, not rejection that would lead to more rejection, fear, and bondage, or death in case of abortion.

It was to begin with a father who would represent God the Father and be the head and key strength of the family. He would love, cherish, honor, and nourish his wife and set the example for his sons and daughter to imitate.

119

As the head he would lead, spiritually and train up his children in the fear and admonition of the Lord. Yahweh has always intended that the father's presence would be felt in every aspect of the home.

Next, the mother would be the heart of the home. She would be lovingly caring, nurturing, training, and encouraging her family, modeling a virtuous woman who fears the Lord and honors her husband.

Finally, children, who understand they are a precious desired gift from God, would then love honor and obey their parents.

That sounds like a perfect world doesn't it? Well, it represents the family as it was designed by God, a family with a solid foundation that would not be fragmented by abortions and all the ills we are experiencing today.

God created this institution, and without His plan everything breaks apart and splinters to a lower form. As the family goes, so goes the culture.

My friend, it is impossible to consider the statistics regarding abortion and fatherlessness and not realize that the family unit is under major attack.

In 1975, Bill Bright, founder of Campus Crusade, and Loren Cunningham, founder of Youth With A Mission both received a message from God that would impact nations for Jesus Christ.

The strategy was to affect the seven spheres or mountains of society with Jesus Christ. Namely those pillars of society are: government, religion, business, entertainment, media, education, and family.

Without question the family is the most fundamental mountain and pillar of society.

Johnny Endow, in his book *The Seven Mountain's Prophecy* firmly establishes that,

Family and morality are the very fiber of order for society. When family order disintegrates, then societal ills and social order also disintegrates because there's a direct correlation between them.

In the seven mountain mandate each sphere has an enemy whose purpose is to destroy the mountain occupants. In the family mountain the enemy is rejection.

It corresponds with the Jebusite nation found in Deuteronomy 7 who opposed Israel. "The word Jebusite means a place trodden down and rejected. That enemy must be disposed if the family is to survive. It is clearly the opposite of love and the spirit of adoption. Rejection is defined as "the refusal to accept, consider, submit to, hear, receive, or admit. "[6] Abortion is the rejection of a child.

However, the family's redemption I believe lies in Malachi 4:5–6 that says,

> Behold, I will send you Elijah, the prophet, before the great and dreadful day of the Lord, and he will turn the hearts of the fathers to the children, and the hearts of the children to their fathers, Lest, I come and strike the earth with a curse.

It's the mantel of Elijah that God will release to defeat the powers of the enemy. Just as the prophet Elijah defeated the prophets of Baal on Mt. Caramel (1 King 18: 17–46) and slaughtered them in the Kidron Valley.

This movement will not only supply love and acceptance but the spirit of adoption which will eradicate the orphan spirt. Roman

8:15 says, "For you did not receive the spirit of bondage again to fear, but you received the Spirit of adoption by whom we cry out, Abba, Father."

I asked the Lord why He chose Elijah for this task and He brought to my mind how Elisha referred to Elijah as his father. Remember! 2nd Kings 11–12 states "As they were going along and talking, behold, there appeared a chariot of fire and horses of fire which separated the two of them. And Elijah went up by a whirlwind to heaven."

Elisha saw it and cried out, "My father, my father, the chariots of Israel and its horsemen!" And he saw Elijah no more. Then he took hold of his own clothes and tore them in two pieces. He also took up the mantle of Elijah that fell from him and returned and stood by the bank of the Jordan and said, "Where is the LORD, the God of Elijah?" And when he also had struck the waters, they were divided here and there; and Elisha crossed over. Elisha then continued the task Elijah began.

That is the same mantel that the Elijah generation will possess in these last days. The Elijah mantel with a breaker anointing to overthrow the Baal god and part the waters releasing resurrection life to the family mountain and nation, thus enforcing Jesus's victory on the cross.

Continuing with the seven mountains that influence society and arguably the family is the most important. Each mountain is ruled by a demonic prince, and for the family it's Baal. Ephesians 6:12 says 'we wrestle not against flesh and blood, but against principalities, against powers, against the rulers of the darkness of this world, against spiritual wickedness in high places.'

Further clarity tells us that *Baal* means "master," "owner," or "lord." He was looked to as god of everything. Service to the god

Molech was also connected with Baal worship, as we see in Jeremiah 32:35. They built the high places of Baal which are in the Valley of the Son of Hinnom, to cause their sons to pass through the fire to Molech. [7]

This was against God's first and sixth commandments. Thou shall have no other god before me and thou shall not murder. It was idolatry and murder. In other words the parents placed their babies in the arms of the god Molech and set fire to them as a sacrifice. Then danced and celebrated their offering. This act represents today's abortions. No doubt!

According to the Alan Guttmacher Institute, research arm of Planned Parenthood, 75 percent give the reason that the baby would interfere with work, school, or other things.

Sounds like idolatry, doesn't it? Yes, sacrificing our babies to the idol gods of this world.

Thus, Elijah's victory over Baal prophets on Mt. Caramel (1 King 18: 17–46) is very significant because it sets a precedence of *faith*, holiness, and victory for the Elijah company today, a victory to return the fathers to their children and children to their fathers, heal the family, and end *abortion*.

The Elijah generation today must arise and ask the same question to this nation the prophet Elijah asked Israel. How long will you halt between two opinions? If God be God serve Him If he be Baal serve him.

The confrontation on Mt. Caramel had two altars: one for Baal and one for the Lord. The one who answered by fire would be god. Remember Baal wanted child sacrifices.

The prophets of Baal begged for a response but none came from their god all day long. Then Elijah repaired the altar of God and called upon the Lord and the fire fell. The Lord, He is God! Repairing the altar of holiness is always the key to the fire falling.

Also remember that before Elijah went to Mt. Carmel. In First Kings 17 he resurrected a widow woman's child from death. Lou Engle points out that there is a dead generation of fatherless children that needs to be raised from the dead so to speak, and delivered from suicide, abandonment, depression, violence, and despair today. He says it will take a labor of persistent prayer and healing to raise them back to life. [8] Thus, we need God's fire to fall as it did on Mt. Caramel.

Today this nation must also decide who is its god? Will it be the God of Abraham, Isaacs and the Bible or the god of materialism, comfort, selfishness, or sexual pleasures with no moral responsibility, the god who encourages sacrificing your child on the altar of pro-choice?

The altar that says my comfort is more important than the life in my womb is the altar that would trade a lie for the truth eliminating the next generation ultimately destroying the family and foundation of society.

The prophet Elijah prayed on Mt. Caramel that Israel would know that the Lord was God and turn their hearts back to Him again.

That is my prayer as well, that the fire of God would fall on the hearts of people and burn away all false doctrines, philosophies, alliances, and man's reasoning, that they would arise and declare as for me and my house we will follow the Lord.

So let the fire fall oh Lord. Cause the church to become a house of prayer and let the fire of God fall on America from sea to shining sea.

Interestingly, Daniel 12:1, 3, 10 says this will occur in the last days.

At that time Michael, the archangel[a] who stands guard over your nation, will arise...... Those who are wise will shine as bright as the sky, and those who lead many to righteousness will shine like the stars forever 10, Many will be purified, made spotless and refined... (NLT)

In essence, in the last days the Angel Michael will arise to defend God's people, and there will also be purified righteous people living on the earth. I believe they will be people equipped by Elijah revolutionaries to be Gods ministers on earth.

Chapter 11

RIGHTEOUSNESS EXALT A NATION

I call Heaven and earth to witness against you today.
I set before you life or death blessings or cursing.
Choose life so you and your children may live.
Deut. 30:19 KJV

"Righteousness exalts a nation, but sin is a reproach to any people" (Proverbs 14:34).

"When the righteous are in authority, the people rejoice: but when the wicked bear rule, the people mourn" (Proverbs 29:2).

This chapter is written to bring insight to some and a challenge to others how revival and conversion to God's Word transformed nations.

I love the stories in history that tell how a change in people's beliefs brought renewal to a land. Imagine the transformation that could result if this nation regarded the sanctity of life. Wow, think of that!

The righteousness of God always makes a moral difference in a land. I can recall various outpourings that demonstrate this perfectly.

The Welch revival is a great example. It began in 1904 by a preacher named Joseph Jenkins. He had a vision of being wrapped in a blue flame, and this caused his fiery sermons to inspire great excitement among many people. They came from everywhere including a newcomer named Evan Roberts.

Evan was a twenty-six-year-old miner, a religious young man who had prayed for a revival for ten or eleven years. He was dramatically filled by the Spirit of God during one of the services. Then the next nights, he had visions of hell, of Christ's victory over Satan, and of an enormous revival that would save 100,000 souls.

Although not a priest and not very educated, he became the de facto leader of a revival that swept through Wales "like a hurricane," as David Lloyd George put it in one of his editorials. [1]

Evan's visions were unquestionably from the Lord because the entire moral climate of the country shifted. There were countless conversions. Bars closed, the crime rate declined, and business problems subsided.

Many alcoholics stop drinking, and, along with coal miners, crowded into prayer meetings that lasted until 3:00 A.M. The miners would then bathe, eat breakfast, and return back to work that morning.

In fact, G. Campbell Morgan recalled a conversation with a mine manager about profanity. The manager told him, "The miners had driven their horses by obscenity and kicks." Now they can hardly persuade their horses to start working because they no longer use obscenity or kicks. The climate of the mines had been transformed.

The social impact reported that judges were presented with white gloves signifying no cases to be tried. Alcoholism was cut in half, and at times hundreds of people would stand to declare their surrender to Christ as Lord. Within six months, 100,000 souls were converted in Wales.

The often-quoted statement, "as the church goes, so goes the nation," truly applies here. Evan had faithfully prayed for eleven or twelve years for revival fire to fall in Wales. It fell, and the nation was transformed.

Isaiah 64:1–3 states,

> Oh, that you would rend the heavens and come down,
> that the mountains would tremble before you! As when
> fire sets twigs ablaze and causes water to boil, come
> down to make your name known to your enemies and
> cause the nations to quake before you! For when you
> did awesome things that we did not expect, you came
> down, and the mountains trembled before you. [NIV]

Yes, when heaven comes to earth, God breaks bondages, shakes concepts, corrects wrong beliefs, and displays the truth for nations to realign with Him. Then righteousness exalts the nation.

I agree with George Washington, our nation's first president, who said, "It is impossible to rightly govern the world without God and the Bible." I believe Mr. Washington had great insight from the Lord. Actually, he recorded many instances in which there was divine assistance and intervention for our nation.

In fact during the 1700s, prior to the Revolutionary War, prayer became the major instrument of change. It was not widely known but there was a great deal of apathy and a decline of spiritual truth. It was the Spirit of God that brought change through united prayer. The period was called the Great Awakening.

James Goll, in his book *Prayer Storm*, quotes Dr. A. T. Pierson saying,

> "Not many people realize that in the wake of American Revolution there was a moral slump... crime, drunkenness, profanity, rose to alarming levels. Churches stopped growing and began to shrink. Christians were so few on the campuses of Ivy League colleges in the 1790s that they met in secret, like a communist cell, and kept their notes in code so no one would know."

The chief Justice of the United States, John Marshall, wrote to the Bishop James Madison, that the church "was too far gone to be redeemed". Voltaire averred, and Tom Paine, echoed, "Christianity will be forgotten in thirty years."

How did this change? Prayer! Yes, the effectual fervent payer of the saints or the righteous availed much.

A Baptist pastor named Isaac Backus sent an urgent plea for prayer to every Christian denomination in the United States. Fortunately, churches knew there had to be a response due to the condition of the colonies. So the Presbyterians, Methodists, Baptists, and the Moravians all adopted the plan for prayer until a network of prayer stretched across America.

Every first Monday of every month there was a prayer meeting until revival broke forth. It began in Connecticut, then spread to Massachusetts and all the coastal states. Finally, revival burst into wildfire when it reached Kentucky. There were camp meetings every-where. One communion service was said to have 11,000 people in attendance.

Alexis de Tocqueville said when visiting America,

> I sought for the greatness and genius of America in her commodious harbors and her ample rivers—and it was not there... in her fertile fields and boundless for-ests and it was not there... in her rich mines and her vast world commerce—and it was not there... in her democratic Congress and her matchless Constitution—and it was not there. Not until I went into the churches of America and heard her pulpits flame with righ-teousness did I understand the secret of her genius and power.

My friend, as Tocqueville said, "America is great because she is good, and if America ever ceases to be good, she will cease to be great."

America must awaken to the fact that her survival depends on her keeping God as her first love. The Lord does hold the world in His hand and the rise and fall of nations is based on their relationship with God. Isaiah 2:4 says, "He shall judge between the nations, and rebuke many people."

God's judgment in the past toward Sodom and Gomorrah is an excellent example. Their destruction was so complete that there is absolutely no sign they even existed. Tourists in Israel today only view an empty plain where they once stood.

Psalm 33:12 says, "Blessed is the nation whose God is the LORD, the people He has chosen as His own inheritance."

The United States was established as a Christian nation contrary to contemporary views of today. President John Adams proclaimed,

> We have no government armed with power capable of contending with human passions unbribed by morality and religious people... Our constitution was made only for a moral and religious people. It is wholly inadequate to the government of any other. [2]

After reading Mr. Adams' statement, a person must realize that abortion violates the moral standard this nation was founded on and is contrary to the Word of God.

Genesis 1:27 says, "God created man in his own image, in the image of God created him male and female he created them. " Again in Deuteronomy 30:19 the Lord says,

> This day I call heaven and earth as witness against you. I set before you life and death, blessings and curses. Now choose life, so that you and your children may live.

Every life is precious and represents the image of God on earth. Heaven and earth is a witness between man and God whether we choose to value life and blessings or death and a curse.

Therefore, according to Deuteronomy 30, choosing abortion is choosing death and a curse. Also legalizing it in *Roe vs. Wade* can precipitate the judgment of God, the kind that Sodom and Gomorrah experienced.

Wait a minute! Stop, think: could our nation's disobedience cause the blessings of God, His favor and protection, to be withdrawn from us? Consider the climate, and all the fires, floods, tornadoes, hurricanes, and the extreme weather patterns of the last few years. Could this be a result of our sin and turning from God toward our own selfish desires?

We, as a nation, have God's favor and protection only when we obey Him. Otherwise, through national disobedience we allow the enemy to steal, kill, and destroy.

Do these events now serve as a wakeup call?

Over fifty-six million babies have been killed by abortion since 1973 in the United States. That's genocide. Genocide is the deliberate killing of a people who belong to a particular group. Abortion= genocide of the unborn. [3]

It's time for the same urgent plea that went forth by Isaac Backus, the colonial Baptist pastor in 1794 for prayer. He summoned every denomination to fall on their knees before God and cry out for repentance and revival in the nation.

God holds believers in a nation responsible for the sins in that nation! Note the often quoted verse 2 Chronicles 7:14,

> If My people who are called by My name will humble
> themselves, and pray and seek My face, and turn from
> their wicked ways, then I will hear from heaven, and
> will forgive their sin and heal their land.

Please notice that God does not tell the unbelievers in a nation to repent of their ways, but He tells the believers in the nation that if they will humble themselves, pray, seek His face, and turn from their wicked ways, that He will then hear from heaven, forgive their sin, and heal their land.

I therefore repeat as the church goes so goes the nation that we are not fighting flesh and blood but, spiritual wickedness in the second heaven. That's where the battle rages and that requires us on our knees. We need the partnership of the angelic army and the protection of almighty God.

Recently, while writing this book, I asked the Lord why people could not understand that abortion was murder. Actually I had become baffled in the lack of people's ability to consent to this basis truth.

The Lord's answer was "there is a famine for the hearing of the word." Then I was really confused. A famine for the hearing of the word? I replied. You're saying there is not enough word of God available? No, he replied.

The emphasis is not on the Word but on hearing. Hearing the word leads to focus, and then attention and ends in obedience. That's when you really hear the Word—if it results in obedience. Hearing is defined *obedience* in Hebrew.

Naturally I went to the scriptures, and in Amos 8:1–12 it says,

> The days are coming, declares the Sovereign Lord,
> when I will send a famine through the land—not a
> famine of food or a thirst for water, but a famine of
> hearing the words of the Lord people will stagger from
> sea to sea and wander from north to east searching for
> the word of the Lord, but they will not find it. (NIV)

Unfortunately, during the days of the prophet Amos the Israelites did not love, value, or esteem hearing the truth of the Word. So the Lord sent a sleep so the word became sealed to them and they saw the Word but were spiritually deaf to it. They could not hear!

Isaiah 29:10, 13 says,

"The Lord has brought over you a deep sleep: He has sealed your eyes… [13] these people come near to me with their mouth and honor me with their lips, but their hearts are far from me. Their worship of me is based on merely human rules they have been taught."

Therefore, because they did not value God's word in their heart that resulted in obedience, it was sealed and as a curse on the land the truth, could not be heard. Consequently sin and disobedience flourished.

It was during this time that King Jeroboam of Israel devised his own religious system, leading into gross idolatry. He appointed his own priesthood and established his own centers of worship. Regardless of God's word, he did it his way. He led the northern ten tribes into error rather than unite with Judah and worship in Jerusalem.

The Israelites to a degree wanted the truth, but on their own terms. They were not hungry enough to search for it and go to the Temple, where God was. As a result, they could not find [hear] the words of the Lord ever again. How terribly sad!

Has America followed the same process? Do we have a famine of hearing of the word of God? Has the word been sealed and we find ourselves going to and fro searching for the truth but stumbling because our hearts are hardened and are ears are deaf, all a result of devaluing and disobeying the word of God? Are we operating under a curse and are completely ignorant to it?

Let's face it: gradually, the word of the Lord has been edged out of our society with each succeeding generation along with a diminished regard for the Bible.

We have been swayed from the biblical perspective of truth. We have gone from Darwinism to Modernism and now Post Modernism.

Darwinism said science is more important than faith. Then Modernism said that the view of the world and people should be replicable, provable, and tangible or intellect mixed with the five senses.

Now Post Modernism says we must deconstruct former ways of thinking in order to reconstruct a new society. In other words, there are no absolutes; everything is based on cultural opinion.

Is this not an example of spiritual deafness? We have now constructed laws disobeying the real *truth*, which is the word of God.

One New Testament example of spiritual deafness is of the people in Thessalonica who also did not have a love for the truth of the word. 2 Thessalonians 2:11 says the Lord sent strong delusions so they would believe a lie. Actually, He just gave them what they wanted. He left them to their own desires. He took His hand off and stepped back.

Again, The Voice Bible says the same of those in Rome: "Since they had no mind to recognize God, He turned them loose to follow the unseemly designs of their depraved minds and to do things that should not be done" (Rom. 1:28).

Recognizing God and His word is paramount to allowing righteousness exalt a nation and repel the ultimate reproach.

Did you know that during the same time *Roe vs. Wade* became law in 1973, the U.S. Congress passed "the Endangered Species Act," which not only protects 170 different species of plants and animals but also protects their unborn offspring by law. Yet a child in the womb is unprotected. Should we now admit that our nation apparently values a turtle egg more than an unborn baby?

There are stiff fines and even imprisonment for killing cats, dogs, and even trees, but we do not apply the same standard to our unborn children who are our next generation

Roe vs. Wade and its companion case *Doe vs. Bolton* have legalized abortion-on-demand throughout all nine months of pregnancy. Basically because Doe vs Bolton permits *any* health and distress reason for abortion. So, with an abortionist doctor who could object?

Both cases were built on lies. The women at the center of each case now testify they were manipulated to promote a pro-abortion agenda. Both now are pro-life!

It's difficult to imagine that over fifty-six million children have died by abortion. That's the equivalent of aborting every man, woman and child living in Arizona, Arkansas, Colorado, Idaho, Iowa, Kansas, Minnesota, Missouri, Nebraska, New Mexico, North Dakota, Oregon, South Dakota, Utah, Wyoming, and Michigan!

Abortion is the number one cause of death in the United States. Millions of children have been destroyed, as well as the wounding of men, women, and the damaging of family trees.

I believe America has rejected the light from the Word of God so long that we now have grown accustomed to the darkness. Listen to God's call from heaven:

Deuteronomy 30: 19–20

This day I call the heaven and the earth as witnesses against you that I have set before you life and death, blessings and curses. Now choose life, so that you and your children may live [20] and that you may love the Lord your God, listen to his voice, and hold fast to him. For the Lord is your life, and he will give you many years in the land he swore to give to you.

Choose blessings!

Chapter 12

FOR SUCH A TIME AS THIS

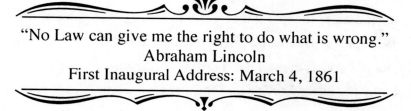

"No Law can give me the right to do what is wrong."
Abraham Lincoln
First Inaugural Address: March 4, 1861

The Lord said In Ezekiel 22:30 that He looks for a man or woman that should make up the hedge, and stand in the gap before Him for the land, that He should not destroy it: but he found none.

During Ezekiel's time Israel had committed sin continually. The broken word of the Lord created a breach between them and God. Ezekiel declares in chapter 22 that the people put no difference between the holy and profane, neither had they showed any difference between the unclean and the clean.... Like wolves ravening the prey, they shredded blood, and destroy souls, got dishonest gain. They used oppression, exercised robbery, and vexed the poor and needy.

However, because of God's great love and the covenant He made with Israel, He looked for a person to stand, and intercede for the injustices and sin committed in the land so mercifully, the judgment listed could be averted. Sadly, He found no one.

Today God's voice is echoing from the throne the wickedness in America. He sees the sin, iniquity, and disregard for His word. Truth has fallen in the street. We have said wrong is right and right is wrong. There is lawlessness and disregard for His authority. Fatherlessness is at an all-time high, and we sacrifice our babies on the abortion altar of convenience to the demon god Moleck.

As an Esther today, I now choose to stand in the gap and ask for forgiveness. I will repent before your throne Lord. We have sinned, dishonored you as creator, God of this earth, and of our lives.

I bow my knees Lord to you and your Son Jesus Christ, and I ask Jesus for the forgiveness His blood paid for on the cross.

2 Chronicles 7:14 says,

> If My people, who are called by My name, shall
> humble themselves, pray, seek, crave, *and* require of
> necessity My face and turn from their wicked ways,
> then will I hear from heaven, forgive their sin, and
> heal their land. [AMP]

Father your word says if we humble ourselves pray and seek your face and turn from our wicked ways, you would hear our voice and heal our land.

- Therefore Lord I stand in the breach and pray before you, and I ask everyone please join me?
- Forgive me (us) Lord for I (we) have sinned. Abortion is murder and a violation of your holy word. I knew your word

but I choose to be silent while millions of babies were aborted in their mother's womb.

- Forgive me (us) Lord for silently complying to the sacrificing our babies at the altar of Molech for financial gain. The abortion *industry brings in $831 million yearly.* It's a business that is about profits far more than it is about women's health. [1]

- Forgive me (us) Lord, because my silence became complicit with the wounding of women and families who could have chosen otherwise if I had spoken truth.

- Forgive me (us) for compromising or agreeing to abortion as an escape from personal responsibility.

- Forgive me (us) Lord for voting into political office those who advocated abortion. In doing that I (we) said wrong was right and right was wrong. I (we) choose political correctness and personal desire rather than honoring you Lord and your Word.

- Forgive me (us) for destroying those you created in your image and likeness thus prohibiting them fulfilling their purpose and destiny on earth.

- Lord I weep and repent for allowing Roe v Wade to make me legally blind to the babe in the womb. Something that is so very important to you.

- Lord wash me (us) and cleanse me (us) with the precious Blood of Jesus Christ for the sin of the shedding of innocent blood and from all of our sin and iniquities.

- Create in me (us) a righteous and clean heart to obey your word. May the blood of Jesus Christ speak louder than the blood crying out from the ground and grant us forgiveness. Forgiveness you paid for on the cross and laid down your life for the sake of a love relationship with us. Oh my. What a love. Thank you Lord.

James 5:16 says:

. . . The effectual *fervent prayer* of a righteous man avails much. The Amplified Bibles puts it this way: "The earnest heartfelt, continued *prayer* of a righteous man makes tremendous power available dynamic in its working."

Now let's all agree in prayer together on these corporate issues:

*Pray:

1. That organizations like the Justice Foundation, founded by Allan Parker, has the wisdom, protection, provision, and access to accomplish successful breakthrough in the court system concerning life issues.

2. That revival would fall in America and the deceptive veil over the eyes of the church would be removed to the horror of the shedding of innocent blood.

3. That the racist policy of targeting black women for abortion ends.

4. That the crisis of fatherlessness would end and the hearts of the fathers would turn to their children and the children to their parents, healing an orphan heart.

5. That people, male and female would be legally blind no more to the unborn.

6. That abortion would not be used as a means of birth control and that sex would be an honorable gift shared between husband and wife.

7. That the child in the womb be legally considered a human person at conception. That the Fifth and Fourteenth Amendments of Constitution would not violate <u>their</u> due process and equal protection under the law as a person.
8. That the connection sex trafficking has with abortion today be broken and victims are not forced to suffer further loss and wounds.
9. That the political handshake with abortion is broken and God's righteous practices established.
10. That *Roe vs. Wade* would be completely overturned.

*Post abortion prayer: For those who have had an abortion and are asking the Lord to forgive you: First understand how much God truly loves you and the exchange He made on the cross between your sin and His forgiveness. My friend, Jesus died on the cross for your sin. He took it. The debt has been paid, and you have been set free. There is no shame, condemnation, no self-hatred necessary. It's over; you're free.

The precious love of Jesus Christ will cover you and cleanse and heals you of any pain with the powerful blood of Jesus Christ.

As the famous Christian hymn goes:

Oh! Precious is the flow that makes me white as snow;
No other fount I know, nothing but the blood of Jesus.
What can wash away my sin? Nothing but the blood of Jesus;
what can make me whole again? Nothing but the blood of Jesus.

It is all about Jesus and His blood that makes the difference. It puts your sin in the sea of forgetfulness. Now forgive yourself.

*Now pray this prayer if you have had an abortion:

Dear Lord please forgive me for aborting my baby. I know now that every child conceived was destined by you for a particular purpose on earth.

I hindered that purpose. Again forgive me; I was blind and selfish to the sanctity of my child in my womb. Forgive me for murder, rejection, and abandonment of my child.

Please cleanse me with your Blood and remove anything that opposes life, and sanctify my body unto you in Jesus Christ name.

*Pray this prayer [If you are a man or someone who contributed to a person having an abortion]

Dear Lord forgive me for contributing to_____ having an abortion. I was selfish and did not honor the sanctity of the baby in the womb. Or as a father I did not protect my family.

I now understand that all life comes from you Lord and you are the only one who can take it away. I was wrong forgive me. I ask you to cleanse me with the precious Blood of Jesus Christ.

I ask you to cause my heart to honor and be a guardian of all life in the womb.

Psalm 127:3 says children are a heritage of the Lord a reward from Him.

I thank you that you are faithful and just to forgive and cleanse me from this unrighteous act. Amen

In conclusion,

To every person reading this book, your personal destiny is too important to allow the act of abortion to separate you from God's loving purpose for your life.

The Lord created the world with laws. They include principle and the consequence if the law is disobeyed. Laws are engrained in nature, our bodies, and the spiritual realm and in all of life. Basically it's life or death, blessings or cursing. Deuteronomy 30:19 says, "I call heaven and earth to speak against you today. I have put in front of you life and death, the blessing and the curse. So choose life so you and your children after you may live."

Perhaps that sounds cruel to you but as the late Myles Monroe said, God created everything for success. Follow the principles or laws, and you'll be successful and you'll reach your God ordained destiny.

I believe our rights actually came from God and they are unalienable, predated and pre-exist the Constitution. Our founding fathers acknowledged that and often patterned much of our constitution after the Bible. Even the Liberty Bell quotes Lev. 25:10 – "Proclaim LIBERTY throughout all the Land unto all the Inhabitants thereof." Therefore how can we the people deny the basic right of **life** to the babe in the womb?

Abortion, regardless of popular opinion, hurts people—women, families, your heritage, the child in the womb and the world. Only God knows what gift was lost by abortion to the world. What if Ronald Regan had been aborted beloved by so many, or President Kennedy even the first African American President Barak Obama. All were ordained to play a part in history just like you and I; abortion would have altered our destiny, family, and this nation.

My *call to action!* *I ask you to choose* life. *Reject abortion and cause every abortion clinic to close for lack of consumers!*

As an Esther, I declare we have come to this kingdom for such a time as this. It's our time to stand, decree life over this nation from the womb to the tomb, reject legal blindness and proclaim — a paradigm shift to LIFE!

"Thank You Father God for
my **life** now on earth."

ABOUT THE AUTHOR
Barbara Grier

Barbara J. Grier is a graduate of Central State University in education and a Detroit Public-school educator for over 30 years.

She served on the Board of Directors and founded the Joy of Jesus Girls inner city camp. Barbara also established Understanding God Bible classes in many local churches.

She is a certified Michigan Model for Comprehensive health trainer and Trainer of trainers. Certified Teacher of Human Reproductive Health.

Barbara is an ordained minister and Community Service Chaplain.

Founded in 1984 by Barbara the Daughter of Sarah Ministries is known for equipping and empowering women, and the Destiny life Network promotes abstinence and prolife. Barbara host a weekly radio broadcast The Voice of Reason on 1440 AM Detroit. She passionately advocates for life, and connects with pregnancy centers in Michigan where she resides.

Barbara is apostolically aligned and is a teacher and conference speaker nationally and internationally known for a breakthrough anointing.

She is surrounded with a loving family of brothers and sister and a host of nephews, nieces and precious godchildren.

Contact: dosministry@gmail.com;
Daughters of Sarah Ministries,
P.O. Box 3196 Southfield Mi. 48037

ENDNOTES:

Introduction
1   The Planned Parenthood Racism Project. "Racism." *Live Action.*
    n.d. www.Liveaction.org

Chapter 1
1   Rites of Life. "The Scientific Evidence for Life Before Birth."
    Zondervan. Web. 1983

2   Justice Harry Blackmun. "The 1973 Supreme Court Decisions on
    State Abortion Laws: Excerpts from Opinion in *Roe vs. Wade*,"
    in *The Problem of Abortion*. Ed. Joel Feinberg 2nd ed. Belmont,
    CA: Wadsworth. 1984

3   Lawrence B. Finer. "Perspectives on Sexual and Reproductive
    Health." 37(3); 110–118 2005. http://www.guttmacher.org/pubs/
    psrh/full/3711005.pdf

4   Subcommittee on Separation of Power. "Human Life Bill." *Open
    Library*. Web. n.d. https://openlibrary.org/books/OL3140411M/
    The_Human_Life_Bill—S._158

5   Scott Klusendorf. "Case for Life." Life Training Institute,
    P.O.6381 Colorado Springs, CO 80934. ©2009–2012.–http://
    www.caseforlife.com/oneissue.asp

6   The Constitution of the United States. Article I. Section Paragraph 3. Web. n.d. ,http://www.constitution.org/constit_.htm

7   *Dred Scott vs. Stanford.* n.d. 60 U.S. 36. Web 1857. http://www.ourdocuments.gov/doc.php?flash=true&doc=29

Chapter 2

1   Chuck Pierce, Rebecca Wagner Sytsema, *Prayers That Outwit the Devil*, California: Regal Books, 1982

2   Francis J. Beckwith, and Gregory Koukl. "Seven Fatal Flaws of Relativism." *Perspective Digest.* http://www.perspectivedigest.org/publication_file.php?pub_id=191&journal=1&type=pdf

3   Chuck Pierce. *Future War of the Church.* California: Regal Books, 2001.

4   " Nearly 13 of Detroit Pregnancies End In Abortion." *WXYX Detroit News* May 22, 2014. http://www.wxyz.com/news/region/detroit/nearly-13-of-detroit-pregnancies-end-in-abortion

5   Joe Vince. "Michigan Sees Nation's Biggest Jump in Abortions: Survey." *Detroit News.* June 8, 2015

6   Justice Antonin Scalia. Speech at Woodrow Wilson Center for Scholars. CFIF. Washington, D.C. Web. March 14, 2005. http://www.cfif.org/htdocs/freedomline/current/guest_commentary/scalia-constitutional-speech.htm

7   Josh M. Shepherd. "Whats Ahead After Losing Justice Scalia, 5 Questions With Prolife Legal Advocate Allan Parker." February 17, 2016. http://bound4life.com/blog/2016/02/17/whats-ahead-after-losing-justice-scalia-5-questions-with-pro-life-legal-advo-cate-allan-parker/

Chapter 3

1 Keith L. Moore. *The Developing Human Clinically Oriented Embryology*. Ed. T.V.N. Persaud. 6ᵗʰ Ed. Saint Louis, Missouri: W. B. Saunders Company, 1998.

2 Franklin Foer. "Fetal Viability." Slate. n.e. 1997. http://www.slate.com/articles/news_and_politics/the_gist/1997/05/fetal_viabilit.htm

3 Gregg Cunningham, Esq., "Why Abortion is Genocide," Abortion Articles. 2010 http://www.abortionno.org/wp-content/uploads/2012/06/whyabortionisgenocide.pd

4 Walter B. Hoye, II. "A New Morality Code." Issues for Life Foundation.

Union City, California. www.issues4life.org

Chapter 4

1 *American Heritage Dictionary*. Houghton Mifflin Harcourt. 4ᵗʰ Ed. 2000

2 Kevin J. Conner. *The Tabernacle of Moses*. Pg 14. Portland, Oregon: Bible Press, copyright 1975

Chapter 6

1 Karen Pazol et al. "Abortion Surveillance –United States 2011." Centers for Disease Control Prevention. November 28, 2014. http://www.cdc.gov/mmwr/preview/mmwrhtml/ss6311a1.htm

2 Guttmacher Institute. "Induced Abortion in the United States." http://www.guttmacher.org/pubs/fb_induced_abortion.html

3 "2012 File of Reported Induced Abortions Occurring in Michigan." Division for Vital Records & Health Statistics. Michigan Department of Community Health. http://www.mdch.state.mi.us/pha/osr/annuals/Abortion%202014.pdf

4   "2012 File of Reported Induced Abortions Occurring in Michigan." Division for Vital Records & Health Statistics. Michigan Department of Community Health. http://www.mdch. state.mi.us/pha/osr/annuals/Abortion%202014.pdf

5   Edwin Black. "Eugenics and the Nazis—The California Connection. Safegate. November 9, 2003. http://www. sfgate.com/opinion/article/Eugenics-and-the-Nazis-the-California-2549771.php

6   "Definition of Institutional Racism." Chegg, Inc. Chegg.com

7   Mensa Otabil. *Beyond The Rivers of Ethiopia*. Bakersfield CA: Pneuma Life Publishing, 1993

Chapter 7

1   CDC Centers for Disease Control and Prevention, "Sexual Risk Behaviors: HIV, STD, & Teen Pregnancy Prevention." CDC. Atlanta, GA, www.cdc.gov/healthyyoth/sexualbehaviors/index.htm

2   David Barton. *Original Intent Book: The Courts, The Constitution & Religion*. pg 324. 5th Ed. Aledo, TX: Wallbuilder Press, 2011

Chapter 8

1   Lynne Sajna, *Destinies Denied: The Spirtual Consequences of Abortion*. Bloodline Publication, 1995

2   Paul Nowak. "Fifteen Year-Old Girl Dies After RU 486 Abortion in Detroit, Michigan," *LifeNews.com*. Detroit, Michigan. March 17, 2004. http://www.lifenews.com/2009/01/01/nat-385/

3   Steven Ertelt. Woman Dies-After-Second-Trimester-Abortion at Planned Parenthood." LifeNews.com. Chicago, IL. July 23, 2012, http://www.lifenews.com/2012/07/23/woman-dies-after-second-trimester-abortion-at-planned-parenthood/

4   "Report of the Grand Jury: Gosnell Case." Philadelpia Gov. Philadelpia, PA/2011 http://www.phila.gov/districtattorney/ PDFs/GrandJuryWomensMedical.pdf

5   Dr. Joel Brind. "Breast Cancer Risk and Choices." Pregnancy Center East. 1995, http://www.pregnancycentereast.com/index. php?option=com_content&view=article&id=23&v=1

6   National Cancer Institute, http://www.cancer.gov/types/breast/ hp/breast-ovarian-genetics-pdq, 1994

7   The United States Court of Appeals For The Eighth Circuit, Case No. 14-1891. Appellate Case: 14-1891, Page: 22, Date Filed: 06/03/2014. http://files.ctctcdn.com/891f5977001/bd6772ff-f6cb-4815-89ce-c32c547657d7.pdf

Chapter 9
1   Stephen R. Covey. *The 7 Habits of Highly Effective People.* Fireside, 1990. P. 67

2   Norma McCorvey's testimony before Congress in 1998. "The 25th Anniversary of *Roe vs. Wade*; Has it Stood the Test of Time?"; Hearing before the Subcommittee on the Constitution, Federalism and Property Rights of the Senate Judiciary Committee, 105th Congress, 2nd Session, January 21, 1998. http://www.endroe.org/ mccorveytestimony.aspx

3   Affidavit of Norma McCorvey. "McCorvey vs. Hill." U.S. District Court for the Northern District of Texas; Dallas Division, Civil Action No. 3–3690-B and No. 3–3691-C. June 11, 2003

4   Norma McCorvey's Testimony Before Congress. Endroe. 1998 http://www.endroe.org/roebio.aspx

5   Norma McCorvey (with Gary Thomas), *Won by Love.* Nashville:Thomas Nelson Publishers, 1997

6   Sandra Cano Affidavit. The Justice Founation. http://thejus-ticefoundation.org/wp-content/uploads/2011/10/Sandra-Cano-Affidavit.pdf

7   United States Court of Appeals for the Eighth Circuit Court. Mirror/Abortion Survivor-Amicus. Arkansas. 8th Case No. 14-1891. http://master-of-photography.us/transfers/2014/Roe-v-Wade_AR/Appeal/Dkt-Mirror/abortion-survivor-amicus.pdf

Chapter 10

1   National Fatherhood Initiative . *"Father Facts."* 6th Ed. Germantown, MD., 2011

2   "Father Factor." Powered by: Launchblot Media, LLC. www.fatherhood.com. 2009-2016

3   Jay D. Teachman. "The Childhood Living Arrangements of Children and the Characteristics of Their Marriages." *Journal of Family.* Issues 25. January 2004, 86–111.

4   Jones RK, Finer LB and Singh S, *Characteristics of U.S. Abortion Patients 2008*, New York: Guttmacher Institute, 2010.

5   Child Trends' Calculations From Data Presented in: Kost, K. & Henshaw, S. 2014. "U.S. Teenage Pregnancies, Births and Abortions." "2010: National and State Trends and Trends by Age, Race and Ethnicity." Guttmacher. http://www.guttmacher.org/pubs/USTPtrends10.pdf

6   Johnny Enlow. "Jebusites And The Mountain of Family." Reclaiming the Seven Mountain of Culture. Web. Copyright 2007 http://www.7culturalmountains.org/apps/articles/default.asp?articleid=39120& columnid=4335#sthash.mEXYCY3Y.dpuf

7   Johnny Enlow, *The Seven Mountain Prophecy and the Coming Elijah Revolution.* Chapter 11. Lake Mary, FL.: Creation House, 2008

8   Lou Engle and Sam Cerny. "A Moment to Confront," The Call Inc. Pasadena, CA, 2011

Chapter 11

1   The Welsh revival: mass hysteria or outpouring of grace? Jules Evans, Ed. Web http://philosophyforlife.org/the-welsh-revival-mass-hysteria-or-outpouring-of-grace/#sthash.kvxTBFqL.dpuf. June 7, 2013

2   Charles Frances Adams. "The Works of John Adams, Second President of the United States." Ed. Boston: Little, Brown & Co.. 1854, Vol. IX. P.229. To the Office of the First Brigade of the Third Division of the Militia of Mass. Pg. 342. October 11, 1798.

3   Office of the UN Special Adviser on the Prevention of Genocide. OSAPG Analysis Framework. http://www.un.org/en/preventgenocide/adviser/pdf/osapg_analysis_framework.pdf.

Chapter 12

1   "Abortion for Profit." n.d. http://www.abort73.com/abortion/abortion_for_profit/

CPSIA information can be obtained
at www.ICGtesting.com
Printed in the USA
FFOW05n2016280316

9 781498 466943